IT IS YOUR TIME TO FOLLOW ME

Dear Steve,

I know you love to read
so I do hope you find this
book inspiring, challenging,
encouraging & hopeful.
"He is risen indeed! Hallelujah."
Easter 2024

Anthea x

IT IS YOUR TIME TO FOLLOW ME

A RADICAL SALAFI MUSLIM ENCOUNTERS JESUS

THOMAS SAMUEL

i2 MINISTRIES

When I first met Thomas Samuel, I could see that this was a man who had met Jesus. In subsequent conversations with him, I became keenly aware that God intended to use him for kingdom work. I wholeheartedly commend this book to those who want to understand Islam better and see how the power of Christ can transform committed Muslims into powerful servants of our Savior!

— MIKE LICONA

Thomas Samuel (not his given name) was raised to be a martyr for Islam. He hated Christians and Jews, because he was taught to do so...and then Jesus got hold of him. What an honor it is to recommend Thomas' book, *It Is Your Time To Follow Me*. In an age of hopelessness, his story is a reminder that God has not forgotten us, He is still at work, and He is saving even His most hardened enemies from their destructive paths. In many ways, the future of our world will turn upon stories like that of Thomas.

— DANIEL BRUBAKER

I love reading conversion stories and seeing how God uses specific and often very particularized pathways to bring people to Christ. So, it was a great joy to read Thomas Samuel's narrative and how God used his Muslim background, his doubts, his rebellion, his visions of Jesus, and Christian apologetics to bring him to where he is today. I pray that God will use Thomas's story to point many to Christ so that they too might realize that "it is your time to follow me" —or simply that believers would be encouraged in their Christian faith and in sharing Christ with Muslims.

— PAUL COPAN

PRAISE FOR THOMAS SAMUEL

Thomas takes us deep into the heart, head, and hand of modern Islam. His passion for the cause of Islam has been transformed into a passion for the Lord Jesus Christ... and this wonderful book takes us on this compelling journey with Thomas Samuel. Glory to Jesus!

— PAUL BLACKHAM

Typical, though grippingly unique story of the conversion of a Salafi Imam, from Islam to Christ. The author's experience contains all the struggles that a Muslim faces when confronted with the powerful message of the Gospel of Christ, which furnishes a compelling comparison with all other alternatives, not least Islam. It also demonstrates how the Comforter (he who gives strength) supports a convert's arduous journey of fellowship of Christ, replacing their sadness with joy and their losses with infinite riches in Christ. Best read of the year.

— EMIL SHEHADEH

Thomas Samuel's beautiful testimony puts to rest the claim that no true Muslim scholar ever becomes a Christian. People of all faiths will find much here to encourage and challenge them in this very thoughtful and personal account of a Salafi Imam's life-changing encounter with the Gospel of Jesus Christ.

— JOEL RICHARDSON

Can God save a fundamental extremist Muslim? And how can that happen? This book is a testimony to the power of God that penetrates a heart of stone and turns it into a heart of flesh, a heart after God. Read this amazing testimony and share it with others for their encouragement and for the glory of God.

— GEORGES HOUSSNEY

I appreciated how Thomas weaved apologetics into his testimony, defending the truth about Christ and the Gospel while sharing his story of transformation. We gain insights into our own theology as we accompany Thomas on his quest for the Truth. A fascinating read!

— MARK BIRD

While I have worked for thirteen years in Egypt, I have not met a convert to Christ with the same knowledge of the Quran and a deep understanding of the Sharia as Thomas Samuel. After I got to know him in person, I also got to know his deep devotion to the Lord Jesus. Thank you, Thomas, for this book, it will help many to a fuller understanding of Islam and the questions and struggles that a convert from Islam has to face. I pray this book will help many believers to share their faith with Muslims.

— LARS MÖRLING

I could not put this book down. In fact, I kept interrupting my wife to share with her about Thomas's story! This is one of the most compelling conversion stories I have heard in a long time. It is honest, interesting, and thought-provoking.

— SEAN MCDOWELL

For the memory of Nabeel Qureshi, whose example inspired me. I look forward to meeting him one day.

FOREWORD

Sometimes I read a book and then move on with my life. Other times, a book stays with me, makes me think, and inspires me to share it with others. *It is Your Time to Follow Me* is such a book. It moved me so deeply that I couldn't put it down!

I first heard about Thomas Samuel from a friend. While his story initially intrigued me, I had no idea how powerful it would be until I started diving into the pages of this book. I can honestly say that his story is one of the most moving accounts I have ever read. Period. It is a story of devotion, courage, and transformation. Why did I enjoy it so much? A few things stand out.

First, it is *unexpected*. As you will discover in the pages of this book, Thomas is one of the least likely people we might expect to become a follower of Jesus. He had every reason not to believe. It would cost him personally and professionally. It would put his life at risk. Given his background and radical devotion to Salafi Islam, no one would expect him to give it all up when he encountered Jesus. And yet it happened.

Second, it is *encouraging*. My life experience is completely different than Thomas's. I grew up in a safe, loving Christian home. My father is a Christian apologist. Compared to many people in the world, it hasn't cost me much to follow Jesus. And yet this book deeply encourages me to think about some vital questions: How much am I sacrificing for truth? Do I really live out what I believe? Am I living a courageous life? No doubt, this book will encourage you to wrestle with these questions too.

Third, it is *thoughtful*. Not only does Thomas take us along for the ride of his journey from radical Salafi Muslim to Christian–with stints through atheism, deism, and New Age–but he also offers his reasoning along the way. In other words, he lays out his journey through these worldviews *and* his reasons why he ultimately finds Christianity compelling. You will enjoy his journey *and* be able to assess his arguments for yourself.

Finally, it is *interesting*. Whether at the dinner table, or driving my kids to school, I kept sharing stories from this book with my family. His interview went viral when we discussed his story on YouTube. People hear about his conversion, and quite naturally, want to know more! Even if you are not a Christian, and you are not convinced by his case, you will undoubtedly find his journey fascinating and his life compelling. *It is Your Time to Follow Me* is a moving, human account of how Thomas Samuel was transformed. Trust me, you will enjoy it.

It is truly an honor for me to write the foreword for this book. I hope you will read it, post your thoughts online publicly, and then share the book with a friend. *It is Your Time to Follow Me* is one of the most memorable books I have read in a long time, and I hope it gets the wide readership it deserves.

Sean McDowell, Ph.D.
Professor, Talbot School of Theology and Biola University

PREFACE

We are living in days of great glory and terror, days of miracles and martyrdom. More Muslims are coming to know Jesus Christ than at any other time in history. Multitudes of other Muslims are quietly being radicalized in hundreds of organizations, dreaming of the day when the Islamic Caliphate will, again, rule the world! Even so, the House of Islam is in turmoil. Ours is the first generation in history in which Muslims have access to information that challenges the idealistic view of Islam, the Quran, and Muhammad. Social media is bringing the horrendous acts of radical Islamist groups like ISIS and Hamas into the pockets of hundreds of millions of young Muslims, causing them to search for answers from the first period of Islam. Many times, secret Google searches help them find information that begins to shatter their Islamic worldview, causing them to be open to the Gospel. Simultaneously, others find charismatic Muslim clerics who galvanize their Islamic faith and radicalize their minds against Christians and Jews. Through it all, neutrality is evaporating.

A constant cycle of civil unrest, war, poverty, and oppression by the heavy hand of Islamic regimes have contributed to a sense among many Muslims that cultural norms are crumbling. Governments in a number of nations are pressing harder than ever to nationalize the next generation as a means of retaining control.

Today, we are witnessing, as my Harvard professor Samuel Huntington foretold, the *clash of civilizations* as previously distant worldviews meet head-on through globalization technology. In terms of conversion, the door is swinging both directions; Muslims are becoming Christians, and Christians are also becoming Muslims. But one thing is clear: The LORD is sovereignly driving history to a very defined conclusion—the universal worship of His darling Son, Jesus Christ, emanating now from every tribe, tongue, people, and nation.

From a biblical standpoint, it is also very clear that the church will be victorious if we stay vigilant in the Great Commission (Matthew 28:18-20; Mark 16:15). We don't have a money problem; the global church has 55% of the total wealth—more than Muslims (8%), Hindus (3.8%), or Jews (1.1%). Fully 25% of the Christian church's global wealth is located in one country, the USA. Nor do we lack people. There are today 2.5 billion self-identified Christians in the world, among whom are about one billion Evangelicals and Pentecostals.

In other words, we *don't lack anything to finish the mission—except for our participation.* By 2053, about one-third of the world is projected to be Christian, one-third Muslim, and one-third *everyone else.* The single biggest spiritual battle for the souls of mankind, therefore, will be between Christianity and Islam. **The biggest problem in the world is not radical Islam, it is nominal Christianity!**

The LORD of all history wants every ear to hear the glorious Gospel and every soul to reckon with the person, identity, death, resurrection, and soon return of Jesus Christ.

Thomas Samuel's story is all about Jesus and his saving power. It's about the LORD's desire that none should perish, but that all would have an opportunity to hear the glad tidings of the Gospel, and to respond.

Growing up in a radical Salafi Muslim family, Thomas memorized the Quran and lived a life propagating Islam until Jesus encountered him in the midst of his utter desperation. His testimony provides a window into the Islamic soul that Jesus is gazing upon with his eyes like jealous flames of fire. The LORD of glory desires to redeem the lost souls away from the decaying house of Islam. When you read Thomas' story, I expect your heart to be moved: Jesus made his great Name known to a very unlikely individual.

In a vastly different context, I grew up in a totally non-Christian home in Seattle, Washington. But just like Thomas, I was lost and on my way to Hell. My father was a leading record promoter for the Rolling Stones (London and RCA Records) and other rock bands. I grew up around casinos, bars, poker games, and the like. All of that changed when one man shared the Gospel with me when I was fifteen years old.

I entered the University of Washington in 1990. I was eighteen. As a zealous freshman, I walked through my campus sharing the Gospel as God gave me opportunities. One day I noticed a very tall black man wearing a long white robe and a skull cap. I said to myself, "This Muslim man has to be the scariest person to share the Gospel with!" However, I reasoned, Jesus loved and died for me, a nobody from nowhere, so I decided to share the love of God in Christ with him!

When I shared with him about Jesus, his reaction astonished me. He fired back in rapid succession: "Your Bible is corrupted, and your New Testament is untrustworthy. How is it possible for God to have a son? Who was God's wife? Did God have sex to have a 'son?' This is an animal act. When God died on the cross, Jesus died, so who was running the universe? Jesus was never crucified. Where does Jesus ever say in the Bible, 'I am God, worship me?' How can God be three and one at the same time? If Moses wrote the Pentateuch, why did he die in it? How can a dead man write his own book? The Bible is corrupted: The endings of Mark 16:9-20 and 1 John 5:7-8 and the story of the adulterous woman are all missing from your early manuscripts. Islam is the straight and narrow path. Muhammad is humanity's final prophet. Islam is the best of all religions. Muhammad is mentioned in the Bible hundreds of times! Every Qur'an is identical; not a single letter, dot, or vowel varies from East to West, a matchless miracle preserved by Allah. Islam encompasses a complete way of life. The Holy Quran is a scientific marvel unchanged and un-variant from the original. Islam is simple and straightforward, in contrast to all of Christianity's contradictions, and has failed as it has produced an immoral Western society."

As I walked away from that encounter, I realized that I had no idea how to answer him. And as I prayed and reflected, I felt God calling me to learn all I could about Islam to train the global church to evangelize the Muslim world *in this generation.*

So I began to study Islam, and doing so, I became shocked! Why was no one talking about the Muslim challenge? At that time, there were 860 million Muslims in the world, and they were by far the largest unreached peoples on the planet. For every Mormon or Jehovah witness there were 100 Muslims in the world! I supposed that there must be entire Bible schools in every country dedicated to addressing this enormous challenge.

I was wrong. Global Christianity was not, as a whole, taking the challenge of Islam seriously at all. I had to study at six different universities in order to learn under the right professors. By the end, I had learned a lot—maybe even too much! I had to read outside of the traditional courses and read into the Islamic Sources themselves and critical studies on Islam and Christian theology. I felt prepared personally to deal with the Muslim challenge. But what about the other 1 billion born-again Christians across the globe? The Assemblies of God, the Baptists, Foursquare, Church of God, the Presbyterians, and so forth?

Some of my most important lessons sunk in during the breaks between class terms. Over the summer months, I would go to Alaska and work on commercial fishing boats to pay off my student debt. Laboring as a fisherman in the dangerous northern waters, I experienced what it was like to catch a million pounds of salmon in just a few months.

I did this every summer, working with a fleet of boats under a high level of organization and using technology to locate the schools of fish in order to harvest an entire sea. It took the fleet captain years of experience to understand the challenges and threats of the sea, how to train the crews, how to coordinate the boat positions, and how to use the right equipment to get the job done. When the fleet worked well together, the amount of fish we hauled in was beyond comprehension and provided almost enough to feed the entire world.

This experience painted a vibrant picture for me of what Jesus meant when he called us to be *fishers of men* (Matthew 4:19).

Twice, Jesus showed us His definition of fishing through the miraculous catches of fish (Luke 5:1-11, John 21:1-14). I believe that those miracles were prophetic, representing and explaining to us the kind of harvest He will bring in if the global church obeys His call to launch into the deep and cast our nets into the 'impossible' waters.

Since 2003, my team, my wife, and I have traveled to approximately fifty countries (some twenty times) for the purpose of training and mobilizing the largest Christian denominations and church networks.

Everywhere, I have observed the same trends. Christians the world over think Muslim ministry is *someone else's calling*, and they are, in general, *skipping the task of evangelizing Muslims*. The 5.5 million local Christian churches seem to be content sending just a few missionaries far away...but they are not setting missional strategies to actually reach all Muslims.

At the time of this writing, the world has about 2 billion Muslims. 86% of those Muslims don't personally know a single Christian. That is *1.7 billion* lost souls! Nearly 40% of all non-Christians globally are Muslims. Yet even today there is only 1 missionary for every 420,000 Muslims. A Pew Research study conducted in 2015 projected that by 2070, Islam could surpass global Christianity as the world's largest religion. Worst of all, about 38,000 Muslims die every day without the Gospel. This situation must change.

Just like Thomas Samuel's amazing testimony of coming to Christ, I have found pockets of great hope. In the last 20 years, I have seen a shift as churches are starting to wake up to the call to reach the Muslim world. Now national churches are willing to train and mobilize like never before. I also know of at least 94 unique movements in the world where 1000 Muslims have come to Christ or 100 churches have been planted among them.

In an effort to train the global church to reach the Muslim world,

I began video recording all the professors I thought were the best on all the essential subjects pertaining to Muslim ministry. By God's grace, we recorded 30 professors and have dubbed them into many languages. 40 professors also contributed articles to what became Mission Muslim World University or MMWU.

In 2020, MMWU launched a pathway to an online master's degree in Christian Ministry with an Islamic Studies Concentration, and we found a way to offer national leaders from around the world scholarships into the program.

It was in MMWU that I had the great privilege of meeting Thomas Samuel. We were able to offer Thomas a full scholarship, and he did not disappoint us. Quickly it became evident that Thomas was a man of great character who was called by God, anointed, sharp, scholarly, evangelistic, and diligent. Thomas graduated from MMWU and God's Bible School and College with an MA degree in Ministry with an Islamic Studies Concentration and is now working towards a Ph.D. in Christological Monotheism and Trinitarianism.

Thomas Samuel was once a radical Muslim, full of hatred and destined for eternal fire. However, God is so rich in mercy and abounding in love that He reached down and saved him in an astounding way. Thomas' journey to Christ outlines the extremely difficult road Muslims around the world have to walk to find hope and freedom in Jesus. The journey this man has had to go on to get to where he is today has been beyond difficult and puts the grace of God on display in profound ways.

Thomas was forced to make a decision to follow Christ that cost him everything, but if you ask him, he will say what he received in Christ far surpasses all that he had to sacrifice. This story tells how he wrestled through the cost of following Christ to the point of almost losing his mind. Thomas had major supernatural encounters that pulled him to Jesus, but like so many others, that wasn't enough. He searched and searched for truth in many world religions before he finally found his rest in God as he studied the vast corpus of evidence for the Christian faith and became discipled by Christians who were willing to take the time to help him.

Thomas is a trophy of God's mercy, and now God is using him in many ways to help the global church cast their nets into the turbulent Islamic waters.

I have walked closely with Thomas for the last 3 years. Despite his background, he is just a normal guy who cracks jokes, likes Indian food, and is trying his best to be a good husband. I have spent countless hours talking to him. But above all, Thomas has labored in prayer and study to fully avail himself to God. And now, Jesus is using his story in beautiful ways. I have seen him in weakness, we have argued, we have laughed. I have seen him fight through very difficult times and have cried in prayer with him as he has persevered in his pursuit of the will of God.

I praise God for bringing Thomas Samuel into our lives. His wife Nancy, who also comes from a Muslim background, is his co-laborer in the Gospel, and together they run the MMWU Arabic program.

I urge you to give his story your full attention, to listen to what the Holy Spirit is saying to you today, and to find your place in the Great Commission.

Joshua Lingel
D.Min., MA, MA, BA
President, i2 Ministries (i2ministries.org)
Dean, MA program, Mission Muslim World University (mmwu.org)

INTRODUCTION

For we did not follow cleverly devised myths when we made known
to you the power and coming of our Lord Jesus Christ, but we were
eyewitnesses of his majesty.

— 2 PETER 1: 16

In 2019, I was asked to write down my testimony. So, I opened a
Word file and sat down with a cup of hot coffee to write. But when I
did so, I found myself at a loss. My mind was blank, and I suddenly
felt unprepared to lay out my life story in this way. Even though I
had previously done so several times on TV, writing it for book
publication is different. For one thing, a book is far more permanent.
Writing this book, I realized, would require a sober readiness to state
my own experience of God's glory in a clear and lasting way. To
borrow the words of Peter quoted above, is time to say to the world
that we did not follow cleverly devised myths when we made known
to them the power and coming of our Lord Jesus Christ.

Readers should know that, for security reasons, I could not share
everything. However, I have written with confidence as I feel God
has led me.

I pray that God will use the story of my journey, with all its pitfalls and mistakes, to be a light on the road that will make Jesus' bountiful mercy and love—that he demonstrated for all to see when he went willingly to death on the Cross—clear yet again and to many people who never understood or experienced it before.

Throughout this book, Bible quotations are from the English Standard Version (ESV), and Quran quotations are from the Sahih International version.

ACKNOWLEDGMENTS

Words cannot fully express my gratitude and joy to be able to accomplish the work that you now hold in your hands. There are many people who are owed my thanks for helping me along on my journey, but I cannot name all of them here. So, I confine my specific acknowledgment to those who helped this book come into the light.

Before all, I thank my wife Nancy who revised, listened, and—even when she was sleepy—worked with me on this book to get it finished on time. She continues to make great contributions in our ministry together. All my love, gratitude and thankfulness, therefore, go to Nancy and also to my family who walk with me on this journey, including its struggles and hardships.

I thank Dr. Joshua Lingel, President of i2 Ministries, and Ryan James who stood behind this work until it came out to the light with all their efforts.

A special thanks should go to Dr. Emil Shehadeh who revised and edited the style of this book to look as it looks today, and to Gwen Montgomery, who did the English proof and fixed my crooked English. Also, a special thanks goes to George Nasser who helped me in footnoting my references. Lastly, I thank Dr. Daniel Brubaker for many final improvements and help with typesetting.

I remain deeply grateful to those professors who gave their review on my book and friends who revised my book before publishing.

CONTENTS

1

HOW TO RAISE A BABY SALAFI

Prepare against them what you 'believers' can of 'military' power and cavalry to deter Allah's enemies and your enemies as well as other enemies unknown to you but known to Allah. Whatever you spend in the cause of Allah will be paid to you in full, and you will not be wronged.

— SURAT AL-ANFAL (QURAN, CHAPTER 8), VERSE 60

My dad was a workaholic who left early to work and came back after I slept, and my mom was the one who raised me with her two sisters. She was a housewife and a very religious woman.

I was a child, around six years old when my mom looked me in the eye and said, "May I see you a leader of this *ummah*,[1] coming with victory, or may I see you dead as a martyr." I will never forget these words. They became part of my psychology and worldview. The passion that I saw in my mom's eyes was too precious for me, and pursuit of these two objectives came to define my life. I wished to please her and make her proud by becoming a leader of the *ummah*, a martyr for Islam, or both.

From the moment my mom spoke those words, my life was changed. Unlike some other children, I did not care much for playing or having fun. Virtually overnight, I became a man on a mission. The more my mom prayed, the keener I became on living up to her prayers.

My family are descendants of Aqeel ibn Abi Talib the brother of Ali ibn Abi Talib, the 4th khalifa[2] of Islam and the cousin of Muhammad the prophet. We enjoyed the status of being Ahl al-Bayt (members of Muhammad's household). So, our roots go back to Saudi Arabia; my great grandfather came—most probably—with the Islamic army when they conquered Egypt and settled in Upper Egypt. Then my paternal grandfather came to live in Cairo when he was in his youth. He was a religious man as well and he raised his kids on deep Islamic religion and faith. It was in this Muslim environment that I had to learn how to pray.

My family insisted on taking me to mosque for prayer. As a matter of obligation, I was made to be present at all family prayers from the age of four. Furthermore, I was expected to read the Quran correctly. Therefore, my family hired a sheikh to instruct me in how to read the Quran.

In addition, I had to learn how to fast. Muslims fast during the month of Ramadan.[3] Radical Muslims may additionally fast on other occasions, such as every Monday and Thursday. Islamic fasting begins at Fajr (the first prayer for Muslims around 5:00 am) and continues until Maghrib (the sunset prayer around 5:00 pm). Accordingly, I was made to fast until Zuhr (the noon prayer). My family would eventually make me fast until ʿAsr (the afternoon prayer), and as I grew older, until Maghrib (the sunset prayer). They rewarded my compliance by buying me presents. In so doing, they were training me that whenever I did something good, I would get a reward, and this was how they believed Allah was dealing with them. So, I learned that Allah was going to reward me whenever I pleased him, which was the foundation of my developing worldview.

Accordingly, I used to perform all the obligatory daily rituals for a Muslim. As if observing the rituals were not enough, I had to memorize the Quran, Sunnah,[4] and what we call "Indisputably established facts of the religion of Islam," which is the road map to a fully compliant Muslim life. This roadmap includes not only the Quran and Sunnah, but also dogmas, daily fiqh (jurisprudence), and the life of Muhammad. This would be done with an immersive attitude which lead to the heart of Islam.

I was seven years old when I watched an Islamic movie about Salah ad-Dīn al-Ayyūbī.[5] The movie represented the hatred that Christianity has for Islam and how Christians want to put an end to all that is Muslim. After the movie, we had lunch, and while we were eating, the doorbell rang! So, my mom asked me to open the door. It was a Christian man, a neighbor of ours called Gerges. I liked Gerges because he was kind and loving.

But, having just watched that movie, I had to ask him, "Why do you hate us?"

So, the man said, "Me?! Hate you! Why? I love you like my son."

I replied, "No, the Christians wish all Muslims to die and desire to take their property."

He responded, "No! Who told you that?!"

I said, "I saw that in the movie of Salah ad-Dīn." The man was astonished, and he did not know what to say.

My mom came out, and she said to him, "He is a kid, and he doesn't know what he is saying."

My mom did not want to have a problem with this man because he rented an apartment from us, and she did not want to risk losing rental income.

However, once the man had left, she said to me, "You are right, I do not want to lose him as a customer, but they do hate us, even though they won't admit it." Subsequently, I began to hate the man and all Christians, because of the way they, apparently, lied to us and pretended to love us while they hated Muslims—us!

Imagine how I struggled with these feelings as a kindergarten child in a Christian school. It was a big challenge for me. That was the only school in our neighborhood which would take a child younger than the minimum age for class.

I was in a minority in my school—one of three Muslim children, to be precise; all the kids were afraid to speak with me about religion or God. It was not easy to always have to leave the classroom during religion periods to learn about Islam. But I was curious as to why we were not all worshipping the same God. I was curious as to why they do not teach the Christian children with us, so they all become Muslims. If Islam is the true religion, why do all people not follow the religion of Islam?

One day, a colleague at school challenged me and said, "You know, you are not one of us. You are not like us because you are a Muslim."

I said, "No, I am like all of you; we are all the same."

She said, "No, and the proof is that you do not have a cross tattooed on your hand like us."[6]

I said, "That's easy, I can do that!" and I took my coloring pen and drew a cross on my hand, not one but many, to convince her that I was not different.

But this was not the end of the story, because when I went back home with all these crosses drawn on my hand, I was so scared. Once my mom saw the crosses, she became so exceedingly angry, more than I had ever seen her before. Full of rage, she slapped me on the face with all her might. I was so stunned that I did not even cry. I was astounded at how angry she was.

She said, "This is your last year at this school. You will be moved to another school next year." And, that is precisely what happened. I was moved to another school with a Muslim majority.

When I asked my mom about the questions that I used to receive from my old classmates at my previous school, she would tell me that Christians and Jews had lost their way. Accordingly, they became enemies of God because Christians say God has given birth to a man, like human beings. Do you think God, who is glorious and omnipotent, can give birth like us? I answered in the negative and added, "But this is too obvious, Mom, so how come they believe that?"

She said: "They believed the devil and denied Muhammad the true prophet of God. That is why we cannot be friends or allies with them, lest we become like them. We deal with them without letting them be close to our hearts except if we can win them to Islam." As the Quran says, "Believers! Do not take the Jews and the Christians for your allies. They are the allies of each other. And among you he who takes them for allies, shall be regarded as one of them."[7]

I was too young to understand everything she said, but I was worried that God would hate me as He hated them. I was taught that Christians and Jews were servants of Satan, and this view understandably served to deepen my hatred of them. Worse still, I was taught that Christian and Jews wanted to prevent the spread of Islam and snuff it out completely. As the Quran said: "Many of the People of the Scripture wish they could turn you back to disbelief after you have believed, out of envy from themselves [even] after the truth has become clear to them..."[8]

Muslims pray five times a day, including al-Maghrib, the sunset prayer. I was eight years old when I decided to postpone this prayer for the first time.

At that time, my mom asked me to justify my decision. "You should go and pray now."

I had no inclination to pray, so I fobbed her off by saying that I would perform that duty later. I simply wanted her to stop nagging me.

But it was time for the evening prayer, which means that I missed the time for the sunset prayer. My mom noticed that too! She stood up, came to me, grabbed me by the hand, and took me to the kitchen. She turned on the gas stove and put my hand very close to the fire. I still remember how painful it was and how my mom was serious about it. Then she said, "If you cannot bear the fire of earth, how will you be able to bear the fire of Hell in eternity?"

I cried a lot! I was so scared, and I felt that my hand would be damaged. That day I learned that God is ready to burn anyone who disobeys. As the Quran says, "On the Day when We will say to Hell: 'Are you filled?' It will say: 'Are there any more?'"[9] Hell was scary for me; I would do anything to avoid Hell.

By the age of nine, my family would allow me to lead some prayers at home, in order to prepare me to lead the prayer at the Mosque. This was part of my preparation process towards a future leadership role in the Ummah (i.e., the global Islamic nation).

My family closely watched news relating to the Muslim world. The idea I received was simple: Islam is persecuted in the whole world; more than fourteen Muslim countries are in a state of war. Therefore, we should grow strong in our religion and convert the world to Islam by da'wa (Islamic evangelism) or by war, because we are right and everyone else is wrong. I learned that Israel is the devil and USA is the devil's servant. We were told that they were behind most events, and Israel represented Judaism and USA represented Christianity. The words of Sheikh Abū Isḥāq al-Huwayni, as recorded in his famous cassette tapes called "al-Mu'amarah al-Kubrā" the great conspiracy, still ring in my ears. He said that America threw away wheat and milk in the ocean whilst one third of the world was dying of hunger. I still remember the title of another cassette tape called "Shar ad-Dawab fi-l-Ard al-Yahud," which means, "The worst beasts in the land are the Jews." It talked about how Jews desired and planned to eradicate Islam from the whole earth.

It is for this reason that Muslims need a leader to unite them and conquer the world. Islam deserves to rule the world—to be in the dominant position and to compel all people from other religions to choose between bowing before Allah or paying the Jizyah (tribute) if they are Christians or Jews. As for all other faiths, they must convert to Islam or be killed, and I believed that this is peace, that when Muslims do that, the world will be more peaceful because there is one religion in control of the public square.

Because I was memorizing the Quran, in the first year at my new school, while I was only in 3rd primary, I was responsible for reading Quran in the Morning school assembly every day. Even the principal of my school used to come every day to hear my voice and to listen to my recitation. The older I grew, the stricter I became in Islam and I kept pace with all the Salafi[10] leaders. At this stage, I did not know whether I was a Salafi or not. But I was persuaded that I had been taught true Islam, and I was a Muslim, who would, one day, give up his life for God and who should become a leader of Muslims; I also noticed that I was following Quran and Sunnah according to the *salāf* (ancestors) of the *ummah* (nation (of Islam)) so I was Salafi even before I recognized it.

---

1. *umma* = "nation," i.e., the global body of Muslims
2. Khalifa or khalifah (Arabic: خليفة): The Arabic word for caliph. It is a title which means "successor," "ruler," or "leader." Khalifa most commonly refers to the leader of a caliphate but is also used as a title among various Islamic religious groups and others. Khalifa is sometimes also pronounced "kalifa." There were four khalifas after Muhammad died, beginning with Abū Bakr, then ʿUmar, then ʿUthmān, then ʿAlī ibn Abī Tālib.
3. Ramadan is the ninth month of the Islamic calendar. Following the example and instruction of Muhammad, it is observed by Muslims as a month of fasting (*sawm* in Arabic) and prayer. Fasting during Ramadan is, in fact, a central tenet of the faith to the extent that it is listed as one of the "Five Pillars" of Islam.
4. The example of Muhammad, as recorded in purported records of his words and actions, such as those contained in the Hadith
5. The Kurdish military commander Salah ad-Dīn (or Saladin, d. 1193 AD) founded the Ayyubid dynasty and subsequently recaptured Jerusalem from the Crusaders at the Battle of Hattin (1187). His rule as sultan stretched across Egypt and Syria.
6. Coptic Christians often used to have a Cross tattooed on their hands.
7. Surat al-Maʾida (Quran chapter 5), verse 51
8. Surat al-Baqarah (Quran chapter 2), verse 109
9. Surat Qaf (Quran chapter 50), verse 30
10. Salafis are members of, or adherents to, Salafism—a movement of Muslims seeking to conform to the practices of the *salaf aṣ-ṣāliḥ*, the pious predecessors or members of the first three generations of pious believers during and after Muhammad's lifetime. The most radical Muslims are Salafis.

2

HIGH SPIRITS

Among the believers are men true to what they promised Allah. Among them is he who has fulfilled his vow [to the death], and among them is he who awaits [his chance]. And they did not alter [the terms of their commitment] by any alteration.

— SURAT AL-AHZAB (QURAN, CHAPTER 33),
VERSE 23

When I was 14 years old, I heard the imam talking, on a cassette tape, about how the *Sahāba*[1] used to carry candles along with them, and that they would burn their fingers after committing a sin, as a reminder of the torment of Hell and motivation not to sin again. Like all my Salafi Muslim teenage friends who were raised similar to myself, and after the example of the *Sahāba*, I carried a cigarette lighter with me so that whenever *I* committed sin, I would burn my finger to remember Hell, and to repent. When the school discovered that I was carrying a cigarette lighter I had trouble persuading them that I was not a smoker and that on the contrary, I had a devout reason for carrying a cigarette lighter. They eventually believed me on account of my reputation as a strict Muslim. It was not an easy life at all!

When my uncle became the imam of the mosque (Arabic *masjid*) next-door to our home, I used to lead the prayer, and he would preach. One day he heard that there was a man who sold alcoholic drinks on our street. Our street was old and serene, most of the neighbors knew one other. I do not remember the man so well, but he was poor and never did harm to anyone. But-, like most of the radical Muslims, we wanted to be in control of our street. Therefore, my uncle decided that this man could not continue selling alcoholic drinks in our holy street.

One Friday, my uncle decided to preach a sermon about the punishment for selling and drinking alcohol. He detailed how this punishment would include witnesses to drinking or selling alcohol who do not do anything about what they have witnessed. As the Hadith[2] says: "Whoever amongst you sees an evil, he must change it with his hand; if he is unable to do so, then with his tongue; and if he is unable to do so, then with his heart; and that is the weakest form of Faith."[3]

By the end of the sermon, when emotions were running high, my uncle revealed the name of this man and reminded us that we are responsible before Allah to stop him and to prevent this man from spreading sin among our people. Then he led around one hundred people out of the mosque to the place where this man was selling alcoholic drinks. They destroyed all his drinks and ordered him to stop selling alcoholic drinks, or they will cast him out of the street. The man had no choice but to comply, or risk losing his life.

When my uncle returned to our house, my mom was so proud of him, welcoming him as if he were a victorious leader of Muslims, coming back from a holy war. I was so proud, too, that we were able to put an end to bad habits in our street and that everyone looked upon us as the representatives of Islam in our locality. I was proud that we have reconquered our street for Allah and restored it to Islam. I felt like the *khilafah* in our street!

Anasheed,[4] that is, Islamic songs, had become a very important part of my Muslim life. The first cassette tape I bought was called "ash-Shaymā Tabki," which means "a girl named Shaymā is crying." The theme of the cassette tape was holy war. The *anasheed* on it highlighted how Muslims were apparently persecuted everywhere and how the world was deaf to Muslim pain and suffering. Such songs, which kept replaying in my head, filled me with hatred for Christians, Jews (whom I considered to be the enemies of Allah), and all those who plotted to thwart our plans for the restoration of Islamic khilafah.[5]

By the time I reached my teens, I was already teaching in the mosque (to teenagers the same age as me), leading the prayer whenever I was available in the mosque, especially on Fridays. People used to come from far away to hear my voice reciting the Quran. Also, I was responsible for what in Islam is called *Ḥalaqet 'Alem*, a circle of knowledge, a group of people learning about religious topics together. After a while I became the head of a circle which consisted of forty-two students. I was teaching them "Islamic behaviors."

The 11th of September 2001 attack on the World Trade Center in the USA is indelibly imprinted on my memory. On that day, I was in my room when I suddenly heard my aunt shouting, "Allah Akbar, Allah Akbar, Allah Akbar," and bowing down to God. We all rushed to see what happened and found out on TV that it was the infamous 9/11 attacks. This day was like a feast at our home; such a glorious day; everyone was jumping frantically out of excitement in celebration of this victory. I was happy, but at the same time, I wondered, is this the victory we were seeking? I was always looking forward to fighting a war, but not killing innocent people such as those whose lives were lost in the wreckage of the World Trade Center. When I expressed my reservations, my mom said: "We are destroying their economy, and this is part of the war; we should destroy their resources at whatever cost because this is the way for Khilafah and for Islam to dominate."

The 22 March 2004 is another memorable day on which the assassination of ash-Sheikh Ahmed Yassin, the leader of Hamas took place.[6] For my strictly Muslim family, this day was as if we were attending a funeral for a family member. Everyone was crying and praying to Allah to bless the soul of ash-sheikh Ahmed Yassin. We also prayed that Allah should destroy the Jews and Israel.

I felt that I had just suffered a sort of personal defeat. Consequently, I wanted revenge. I cried so much and I vowed that I would not stay silent.

At that time when people were exchanging computer hard drives and CDs containing porn among the youth of my Egyptian community, the "Salafi community" also exchanged hard drives and CDs for films of a different kind, which consisted of movies of our group and our mujahideen[7] brothers in Chechnya and Bosnia. We used to hide them, but not for fear of our parents, but rather for fear of the security forces, because the material was smuggled, rendering it illegal. The illegal tapes contained motivational chants such as the tape of ash-Shaymā Tabki ("ash-Shaymā is crying"), as-Sārikh ("the screamer"), and al-Āṣif ("the soft-hearted").

The tapes revolved around two themes:

1. Victory in one of the battles, namely hit-and-run attacks
2. The martyrdom of one of the mujahideen in which he is dying in pain and trying to convince us that he is smiling (because he can see the *hoor al-ʿayn*—beautiful eternal virgins in paradise—and Muhammad's companions, etc.)

One of the anasheed was about a girl who was raped by the enemies and mourning the manhood of Muslims. Another mourned a mujahid[8] who died in the way of God. Another was about lamenting for the armies of Muslims.

The chants were interspersed with excerpts from the sermons of the Imams about jihad or the Islamic State, such as this nasheed that I remember as clearly as my date of birth, which was said in a very enthusiastic voice:

Where are the swords of the Nation,
where are the blades of Khalid, Muthanna, and Tariq,
and has the sword of Salah ad-Dīn become a six-pointed star
hung by a Jewish woman as she treads on the Dome of the
Rock,
saying: O Salah ad-Dīn, stand up if you are brave,

And we are in our disappointment, around the walls of
Jerusalem we are fighting,
through which door shall we enter, which gate shall we
open?
He sold the precious cheaply and fell asleep without a
homeland.
Even tears of sorrow over the cheeks without accom-
modation
He had his joy, and today he is possessed by grief
The enemy broke his sail, and with his hand, the halter was
broken
Oh, the stab of criminality, who hid you from his eyes
The whims of passion tempted him, and the colors of temp-
tation slandered him
Milk watered loved ones and poison mixed in the milk
He cries, and it is useless to cry; oh, what a cruel weakness
What is my trick to the one who sees the ugly as good?
The deceiver's palm behind him, he did not know about his
hand, then
They fear that they know that time has permission
All that they hide one day will come out to the public
The evil of humiliation is kneeling in the crowd to an idol
Who would realize my friend if he was trusted by cunning?

Words stirred our consciences; we wept from disgrace and weakness and were angry and aroused, greedy and aspiring to regain the
place and glory lost to the Ummah.

It was a life other than everyday life, we carried worries prema-
turely, and we grew old in the prime of life and even before the
formation of the entity began...we carried the concerns of a nation,
not just ourselves or our friends and family...we reaped what we did
not sow, and we sowed what others will reap.

In preparatory school, I realized how much more of a Salafi I had
become. I remember the day I listened to one of our imams in the
mosque teaching about da'wah, where we learned that we need to
invite people to our group. Here I started to realize that there is a

clear distinction between "them" and "us." This was the beginning of my perception of "othering" in Islam. We are not one; we are not the same! I had always felt it subconsciously, but had never recognized it until that day.

My schedule was packed with lessons in the mosque five days a week besides the Friday lesson, and only one day off to revise and memorize my lessons. A good memory is essential for an ambitious Salafi; you must know a lot, practice regularly, and stand bold. That is why we were waiting for any opportunity to be witnesses for Islam and make da'wah to liberal Muslims to become Salafi.

Initially, I would da'wah to liberal Muslims as a hobby because my mind was busier with jihad. I wanted to engage in jihad by any means. However, when the second Gulf War, started in Iraq (20th March 2003), something snapped inside me. I was in secondary school full of enthusiasm, energy, and power. But I could not bear it anymore; I could no longer stand the idea of oppression and persecution of Muslims worldwide. Also now, the USA was taking over Iraq, the capital of the Islamic Khilafah, for many years. I decided that it was time to go to war against the USA.

---

1. The contemporary companions of Muhammad
2. Ḥadīth (Arabic: حديث ḥadīth, pl. أحاديث aḥādīth: literally "talk" or "discourse") or Athar (Arabic: أثر, 'athar, literally "remnant" or "effect") refers to what most Muslims and the mainstream schools of Islamic thought, believe to be a record of the words, actions, and the overt or tacit approval of the Islamic prophet Muhammad as transmitted through chains of narrators. In other words, the Hadith are transmitted reports that purport to tell what Muhammad said and did.
3. Narrated by Muslim, in Riyāḍh aṣ-Ṣāliḥīn, Introduction, Hadith 184
4. Anasheed is the plural form of nasheed, which means an Islamic song without music.
5. Whereas khalifah is the person known as caliph, khilafah is the related word that refers to Islamic state (i.e., ruled by a khalifa). Khilafah is the dream and objective of the Muslim world.
6. Hamas (Arabic: حماس ḥamās, "zeal" or "enthusiasm"): An acronym for ḥarakat al-muqāwamat al-islāmiyyah (حركة المقاومة السلامية) roughly meaning "Islamic Resistance Movement." Hamas, a branch of the Egyptian Muslim Brotherhood, is a Palestinian Sunni Muslim fundamentalist organization opposed to Israel.
7. Muslim fighters, that is, those who take part in jihad for the cause of Islam
8. The singular form of "mujahideen," that is, one Islamic fighter

3

DREAM OF A JIHADI

And never think of those who have been killed in the cause of Allah as dead. Rather, they are alive with their Lord, receiving provision.

— SURAT ALI ʿIMRAN (QURAN, CHAPTER 3),
VERSE 169

At the same time, I was both angry and sorrowful because of what I perceived to be our weakness as Muslims, and I wanted to end this pain and suffering. At that time, I came to realize that one of the leaders of a group called *Ansar as-Sunnah al-Muhammadiyah*. Which translates as "Supporters of the Muhammadan Sunnah," was living near my home. I was excited to discover that he had direct contact with the jihadi people in Iraq, which could potentially facilitate or hasten my move to Iraq.

When I eventually got to visit him and discuss my jihadi aspirations with him, I found him supportive.

He looked at me and said, "At last." We need people like you who are strong and eager for Islam and want to make a contribution towards restoration of the Khilafah."

So, I started to prepare, both psychologically and physically, for my dream which appeared more feasible than ever. I was willing to fight for Allah and die for him. I noticed that Muslims were still weak and that therefore my most achievable goal, in the circumstances, would not be victory but martyrdom. As the Quran says, "Go forth, whether light or heavy, and strive with your wealth and your lives in the cause of Allah. That is better for you if you only knew."[1]

Ibn al-Qayyim summarized the development of the idea of jihad in 4 stages:[2]

Stage 1: Before jihad was permitted

Many of the People of the Scripture wish they could turn you back to disbelief after you have believed, out of envy from themselves [even] after the truth has become clear to them. So, pardon and overlook until Allah delivers His command. Indeed, Allah is over all things competent.[3]

Tell those who believe in forgiving those who do not look forward to the Days of Allah: It is for Him to recompense (for good or ill) each People according to what they have earned.[4]

Stage 2: Jihad was permitted

To those against whom war is made, permission is given (to fight), because they are wronged; and verily, Allah is most powerful for their aid.[5]

Stage 3: Jihad as a defensive tool

If they leave you alone and do not fight against you and offer you peace, then Allah does not permit you to harm them. You will also find others who wish to be secure from you and secure from their people but who, whenever they have any opportunity to cause mischief, plunge into it headlong. If such people neither leave you alone nor offer you peace nor restrain their hands from hurting you, then seize them and slay them wherever you come upon them. It is against these that We have granted you a clear sanction.[6]

Stage 4: Jihad as an obligation for Muslims to carry out against all non-Muslims in order for Islam to spread:

And when the sacred months have passed, then kill the polytheists wherever you find them and capture them and besiege them and sit in wait for them at every place of ambush. But if they should repent, establish prayer, and give zakah, let them [go] on their way. Indeed, Allah is Forgiving and Merciful.[7]

O Prophet, fight against the disbelievers and the hypocrites and be harsh upon them. And their refuge is Hell, and wretched is the destination.[8]

Fight those who believe not in Allah nor the Last Day, nor hold that forbidden which hath been forbidden by Allah and His Messenger, nor acknowledge the religion of Truth (even if they are) of the People of the Book,[9] until they pay the Jizya with willing submission, and feel themselves subdued.[10]

And fight them until there is no fitnah and [until] the religion, all of it, is for Allah. And if they cease—then indeed, Allah is Seeing of what they do.[11]

In the Hadith also:

"I have been commanded to fight the people until they testify that there is no deity worthy of worship except Allah and that Muhammad is the Messenger of Allah, establish the prayer and pay the Zakah." (*Saḥiḥ* Al Bukhārī, volume 1, page 95. The same report is also narrated within the other *sunnah* books, with the exception of the collection of Ibn Mājah) (see also *Tafsir Ibn Kathīr* (Abridged))

Then, after a few weeks of impatient waiting, I received a most

disappointing phone call informing me that I could not travel to
Iraq. The whole operation had been canceled due to security
reasons. Two days after this news, the USA invaded Baghdad. I felt I
had lost everything: my hope and my dream to defend a Muslim
country.

Why did Allah permit this to happen? Has Allah rejected me? If
so, why?

A hadith narrated by Abū Hurayra says: "I heard Allah's
Messenger saying, 'The example of a Mujahid in Allah's Cause—
and Allah knows better who really strives in His Cause—is like a
person who fasts and prays continuously. Allah guarantees that He
will admit the Mujahid in His Cause into Paradise if he is killed;
otherwise, He will return him to his home safely with rewards and
war booty.'"[12]

Why was I not permitted to do jihad? Why is it that despite all
the prayers I prayed and the worship I offered to Allah, my fasting,
my teaching of others, and the faith I have, why is it that I am still
not able to do jihad? I supposed that Allah, who in his sovereignty
controls everything, did not permit. Is it not written in the Quran,
"Say: I possess not for myself any harm or benefit except what Allah
should will"[13]

The most basic question I was grappling with, was: Why did
Allah not will me to do jihad, on this occasion? I was extremely
disappointed, sad, and frustrated, and I became depressed since I
had built my life and dreams around the intention of doing jihad,
which was the only guarantee of paradise. I was terrified by the
prospect of ending up in Hell. Living a righteous, devout life as a
Muslim is irksome. It is virtually impossible to keep up the faith
with diverse temptations all around. No one is sinless, and my
greatest fear was that, sooner or later, I was going to fall into sin and
go to Hell. Jihad was my only guarantee to paradise, and my only
warrant of avoiding eternity in Hell.

As time went on, I became gradually more and more secluded. I
started to pray at home, which everyone found very strange since I
had never missed a prayer at the mosque. One of the leaders in the
mosque where I led the prayer enquired about me. This man was

one of the most intelligent people I had ever met, a successful businessman, a master in da'wa (Islamic proselytization), and was the head over the whole territory of the *at-Tablīgh wa-l-Dā'wa* group. He telephoned me and asked for a meeting, to which I agreed.

He asked me, "Why do you want to go to war?"

I said, "Because I tried to kill and be killed for God as the Quran says: 'Indeed, Allah has purchased from the believers their lives and properties [in exchange] for that they will have Paradise. They fight in the cause of Allah, so they kill and are killed. [It is] a true promise [binding] upon Him in the Torah and the Gospel and the Quran. And who is truer to his covenant than Allah? So, rejoice in your transaction, which you have contracted. And it is that which is the great attainment.'[14]"

He answered, "I know, but who said that you are that type of person? We have many who can go to war, but you are the type of person who we need to talk to and teach people. We need you to make da'wa and spread the religion of Allah."

I said, "But I want to die for him."

Then this man said what I think was a prophecy: "Perhaps Allah wants you to live for Him, so that when you talk, many will die for Allah."

This idea appealed to me. It grew on me more and more. After this meeting, da'wa became my focus. It was no longer just something that I would do in my spare time; it became my life's mission, something I felt that I must accomplish.

The first thing I did under this leader was to get myself trained. Let me tell you how Muslims get trained in da'wa. Having myself spent many long hours in training for da'wa, I observe that the Salafi approach to da'wa falls broadly into two categories: the long-term approach and the short-term approach.

The long-term approach has four basic stages:

Stage One: Personal Attachment

In this stage, we would get very personal with an individual. We

would try to make ourselves his friends who care about him, who
follow up with him, and who understand his problems. During this
stage, we would work a lot on building hope and enthusiasm. So,
after listening to the person's problems, we would make great efforts
to encourage him. We would work to make him feel that when he is
with us he is a better person and that he has a family of brothers
who really cares for him and has a close bond with him. We also
worked to create in him the impression that now God is really happy
with him, and that now he is better than anyone who is not in our
group.

Stage Two: Vision Attachment

Part of getting to be our his friends included involving him with
a small group where we would speak at length about the Islamic
dream and how Islam is the solution for every problem. We would
speak nostalgically about the Islamic dream, emphasizing that the
time period of the Sahaba was Islam's golden age, and that if we
could succeed in getting it back it will be like heaven on earth.

Meanwhile, we would try to keep him busy with as many things
as possible. So, he would go along with us to different lessons and
we would get him to hear many of our imams and leaders, especially
the sort of emotional preaching that speaks about Heaven and Hell
or that speaks about being a good Muslim and the privileges that
accompany that status. We would occupy his mind with our
concerns as much as we could. Also, it was very important during
this stage to get him connected to the group of believers closest to
him, and involved at the "Salafi mosque" closest to his home. In
everything, we worked to make it not difficult to meet with us or to
continue in his path toward Allah.

Stage Three: Empowerment

As a Salafi, you are a hunter. You live to hook others to your
group, to get them to be Salafi, and you need to do that without
telling them anything about being Salafi. They will just become a

Salafi, and will recognize that fact in due course. Then, once they becomes part of the group, they are empowered to bring others. We would teach them that this work is one of the most important things that you can ever do, and that if you want to guarantee yourself heaven—which, actually, you cannot really guarantee in Islam—you have to bring more people over to the truth.

This feeling of success when people bring others to the group is powerful and almost intoxicating. It makes you feel victorious. You feel as if you are actually putting up the pillars of the Islamic Khilafah which we all dream about.

Stage Four: Follow-up

After you start to have your own group that you work with and follow up with, we would then keep you part of the whole group. We would continue to follow up with you to see how things are going, and to check whether you need any help. And, this doesn't happen in a stiff and formal way; everything happens naturally and smoothly, as if it is a normal part of life, a daily routine. But follow-up is very important. If not done regularly, we understood that the person could fall away due to being a newcomer who has doubts, or, indeed, for any number of other reasons.

These are the four stages of the long-term approach, summarized from my experience with Salafism. It is difficult to overstate how effective we found this model. It was getting amazing results.

THE SHORT-TERM APPROACH, in contrast, was used with people we do not know well, or in a situation in which we expect not to be able to see the person again. The short approach, in fact, was very easy. We would open discussion into a subject touching upon the person's personal concerns and problems, asking open-ended questions like, "How have people changed these days?" or, "How did life become so tough?" People in Egypt normally like to speak such subjects, and complain a lot about life and circumstances.

Having begun a conversation in such a way, we now had the opportunity to ask this person—whoever he is and wherever we met him—"What is your name?" His answer will let us know whether he is a Muslim or a Christian. If he gives a Muslim name, then we would say a Hadith or a verse from the Quran. Doing so will help us to gain his respect and his attention. Then, I would clarify what I had just quoted, perhaps by using a story from Muhammad's companions or something similar. By doing this, I could often touch his heart and reach his emotions.

If he said a Christian name, the first thing we would say is: "*Lā-ḥawl wa-lā qawwata ʾilla bi-llāh,*" which means "There is no power but from God." This is an expression that people say when there is something sad or to pity.

In response, the person would usually ask, "Why do you say so?"

I would reply, "You do not believe in Muhammad's prophecy?"

He would say, "No! I am a Christian, but I give respect to all religions."

Then, I would say, "Yeah! But accordingly, you do not believe in the Quran," and before he had the opportunity to answer, I would ask, "Have you tried to listen to it?" He most likely would answer, "Yes, it is everywhere in Egypt," to which I would then say, "Try to listen to it with your heart, and you will know."

After that, I would give him either a cassette tape, or a flyer that talks about the greatness of Islam.

Because such conversations could occur anywhere and at any time, it was very important for us to always go out with da'wa tools in our hands so we didn't not miss any opportunity to do da'wa to others.

If we needed to provoke someone, or if we were faced with a well-educated Christian, then we would go straight to five main questions:

1. Jesus: Was he God or prophet?
2. Jesus' crucifixion: Is it truth or lie?
3. The Bible: Is it distorted or not?
4. God: Is He one or three?

5. Christianity or Islam: Which is the last religion?

Out of these questions, one of them—if not all of them—must hit him hard. Certainly, they will get him thinking. Our rule was always, "If I cannot get you to my faith, then I will at least make you doubt your own."

For me, it became a spark in tinder, lighting a fire of desire to spread Allah's word everywhere, with my classmates, neighbors, and literally everyone I met, even taxi drivers. First, I decided to make 'Umrah—an off-season mini pilgrimage to Mecca—which I performed three times. Subsequently, I returned to Cairo, where I was always armed with flyers, cassette tapes, Islamic oil (as perfume), everything possible, which might help me to be able to access the heart of an individual and give them the message of Salafi Islam.

With time, I became adept at reading people, which enabled me to do da'wa more effectively. With the greedy, I spoke more about paradise; with the cowardly and fearful, I mainly talked about Hell. To those who had no friends, we offered friendship and a community. Once I reached a degree of excellence in my mission, I was approached by one of the young leaders in the group, originally from Palestine, who asked if he could work with me. In the beginning, I did not know who exactly we were working for; I thought we were all working for Allah. However, after a while, I got to see that we were working for other leaders. I did not know them in person, but I did know they were not living in Egypt.

My job simply consisted of brainwashing people and persuading them to become part of our group. Then came the role of my leader, who met the new recruit, after which meeting the recruit would just simply vanish. I heard that some recruits left the country to join the jihadi group in other places and others went to jail for a while.

When I went to university, I sought out students who looked like me, and I started to exercise more caution because I was afraid of being arrested. My relationship with this young leader started to weaken, and I focused more on my education, since I wanted to become a *faqih* specializing in jurisprudence. I was doing da'wa to

Muslims in order to convert them from nominal Muslims to Salafi Muslims. I went to the faculty of law, where I could study sharia. Also, my mentor at that time was a *faqih*, a professor of comparative jurisprudence at Al-Azhar University. I was with him most of the time and learned much from him.

After a while, I started to do episodes on TV in a Muslim Salafi channel. Da'wa on TV is very different from da'wa in the street or with friends, as on TV there are different approaches. I was responsible to spread the word of Salafi Islam in English for English speakers, framing it as the modern religion that can help them live their lives in a better way. So, Salafi Muslims may set goals, manage stress, and develop communication skills, leadership skills and all the soft skills needed for life, but they can do these things through their faith and belief as Salafi Muslims. It was an indirect approach; I intended to cause people to become attached to Islam by helping them to make Islam as part of their daily lives. Then, people would live their lives through Islam, and Islam would not be a separate thing.

My use of television in this way was quite effective. In time, it spread out and succeeded to the highest level. My program "Life Choices" was aired on Thursdays at 9:00 pm, which is the peak time for all the important programs in the Middle East.

The only problem I faced at that period was that I did not feel I was fulfilling my mission. Da'wa to Muslims was not enough; I felt that there was something more to do. Considering that my dream was to do jihad, I found that doing da'wa to Muslims was no substitute to jihad, because my converts were Muslims anyway. As 'Uthmān reported in the Hadith, "The Messenger of Allah said, 'Whoever dies truly knowing that there is no God but Allah will enter Paradise.'"[15] I needed to do something more than just bringing Muslims to Salafism. Then, I started to think about what comes after jihad. I recalled the Hadith, "The Prophet said to 'Ali, 'By Allah, if a single person is guided by Allah through you, it will be better for you than a whole lot of red camels.'"[16]

The first idea that occurred to me was the need to evangelize Christians and help convert them to Islam. But the question was: how could I do that? All the Christians in the neighborhood knew me and were afraid to speak to me because I was so religious, and I had never talked nicely to them. So, I needed to find Christians outside of my immediate circle. It dawned on me that the internet could present the best solution to finding Christians. I started to enter internet chat rooms where I hoped to meet them.

Amanda, a nominal Christian girl who lived in America and was trying to find someone to talk to, became my first Christian contact. At that time, I did not really know what nominal Christians were. As far as I was concerned, she was a Christian. It was not hard for me to communicate with her as I understand people easily, and I could discern that Amanda was a girl who needed to feel safe. Since her boyfriend had abandoned her, she had found it hard to trust people. So, this became my key for dealing with Amanda; I had to make her feel safe in Islam.

To that end, in my interactions with Amanda I went out of my way to portray Muslim men as people who keep their women safe. At one point, she said that she was working hard to make ends meet. I told her that in Islam, we keep our women like princesses who do not need to do anything but take care of their families. She was so impressed by that. I met her several times online, and she started to like me and I could tell that she was tracking with all that I had to say. Then I started to present Islam and to say that if she wanted to have such a life, with her own bank account, with love and care and all the things she dreamed about, she needed to be a Muslim. I connected her to the Islamic center nearest her, and she was so excited that she found friends and people who could call her sister. A week after, she became a Muslim and took the name Amira. The mosque leaders put her directly in contact with a guy from Egypt, whom she married within three weeks.

Amanda was not the only one; I was connected with two more girls. One was like Amanda, with a quite similar scenario; the other, named Patricia, was somewhat different. Although she too was a nominal Christian, Patricia was more disposed to Christianity than Amanda had been. With her, I realized that I would need to shake the Christian idea that Jesus is God. I asked her questions like, "How could God be crucified?" "How could God go to the bathroom?"

"How could God be spat on?" "How could people strip clothes off God?" "How could God be father, son and mother?" At that time, I thought Christians believed that Mary (rather than the Holy Spirit) was part of what Christians called the Trinity, because the Quran presents the Christian view that way when it says: "And imagine when thereafter Allah will say: 'Jesus, son of Mary, did you say to people: "Take me and my mother for gods beside Allah?"'"[17]

And I did shake Patricia's faith, as she seemed never to have seriously considered these questions. She struggled with the challenges I presented and began to see that she lacked answers to refute my points. Consequently, she started to lose confidence in the Holy Trinity. She became hesitant in her answers. By contrast, I presented Islam as the default faith for all people; in Islam we believed that all people are born Muslims, as the Hadith says:

> There is none born but is created to his true nature (Islam). It is his parents who make him a Jew or a Christian or a Magian quite as beasts produce their young with their limbs perfect. Do you see anything deficient in them? Then he quoted the Quran. "The nature made by Allah in which He has created men; there is no altering of Allah's creation. That is the right religion" [Surat ar-Rūm (Quran chapter 30), verse 30].[18]

I persuaded Patricia that Islam is more comprehensible and practical. In it, I told her, you can do things to show your obedience to Allah—for example, by performing Islamic rituals. Islam teaches that you can earn your place in heaven by doing good deeds. After a while, Patricia professed belief that there is no God but Allah and that Muhammad is his prophet and messenger.

During the first three months that I pursued such strategies, I brought three Christian girls into Islam. Someone might ask, "Why girls?" For me, I just found it much easier to convince a member of the opposite sex. And, bringing three Christians to Islam boosted my confidence immensely. Now, I felt capable of converting anyone to Islam, even the Coptic Pope of Egypt himself. Certainly, he could not be more complicated than 'Umar ibn al-Khattāb![19] I decided that if I wanted to target the Coptic Pope, I needed to study to be prepared to confront someone of his caliber.

---

1. Surat at-Tawba (Quran chapter 9), verse 41
2. Ibn Qayyim al-Jawziyya, *Zād al-Maʿād*, 2/58
3. Surat al-Baqara (Quran chapter 2), verse 109
4. Surat al-Jāthia (Quran chapter 45), verse 14
5. Surat al-Hajj (Quran chapter 22), verse 39
6. Surat an-Nisāʾ (Quran chapter 4), verses 90-91
7. Surat at-Tawba (Quran chapter 9), verse 5
8. Surat at-Tawba (Quran chapter 9), verse 73
9. People of the Book (Arabic *ahl al-kitāb*) is a Quranic category of people that includes Christians, Jews, and Zoroastrians. Under Islamic conquest, People of the Book are treated differently than ordinary pagans or atheists. Unlike the latter category, who must choose either to become Muslim or to be killed, People of the Book are permitted a third choice, namely, to live in subjugation to the Muslims and in submission to Islamic law, including annual payment of the *jizya*.
10. Surat at-Tawba (Quran chapter 9), verse 29
11. Surat al-Anfāl (Quran chapter 8), verse 39
12. *Ṣaḥīḥ al-Bukhārī*, 2787, Book 56, Hadith 6
13. Surat at-Tawba (Quran chapter 9), verse 111
14. Surat Yūnus, 49 (Q10:49)
15. *Ṣaḥīḥ Muslim* 26, Book of Faith. This hadith is taken as evidence that whoever dies in Islamic monotheism will definitely enter Paradise.
16. Al-Bukhārī and Muslim; *Riyāḍh aṣ-Ṣāliḥīn*, 1379, Book 12, Hadith 4.
17. Surat al-Maʾida (Quran Chapter 5), verse 116.
18. *Ṣaḥīḥ Muslim* 2658b or Book 46, Hadith 34
19. The second Khalifa for Muslims and one of the hard personalities that converted to Islam at the time of Muhammad. No one imagined that he would convert.

4

DO YOU LOVE ALLAH?

O sister of Aaron, your father, was not a man of evil, nor was your
mother unchaste.

— SURAT MARYAM (QURAN CHAPTER 19),

VERSE 28

As an aspiring specialist in Islamic apologetics, my top
priority was now to find appropriate training and sound
sources for learning. I found a suitable training program
with special focus upon Christianity, which was a great starting
point for me. I bought books like *Izhāru-l-Haqq* ("The Truth
Revealed") by Imam Rahmatullah al-Hindī (Years later, after
becoming a Christian, I would write my master's thesis refuting all
the arguments in Imam Rahmatullah's chapter about the Trinity in
this same book), *al-Uṣul wa-l-furū'* by Ibn Hazm, *al-Jawab as-Sahīh li-
man Baddal Dīn al-Masīh* by Sheikh al-Islam ibn Taymiyyah, and
others.

At first, I was so excited as I zealously undertook these studies.
However, my excitement did not last for long: I soon found out that
the sheikh teaching us did not care to dig very deep into these
subjects. I noticed that 80% of the content of his talk was about not

about Christianity, but rather about Christians. For example, he was always speaking about how Christians are unclean, how they do not care if their women go to the hairdresser and let another man touch their hair, which in his opinion showed how Christian men are cuckolds.

This sheikh further taught us that Christians are using numerous means to export Christianity to us through games, songs, movies, and so forth. Only 20% of his teaching was actually about Christianity itself, the content of which—in my estimation—was the heart of the problem. When this sheikh would state that Jesus never said 'I am God,' or that he could not have been crucified, or that God never mentioned that He is triune, in my opinion such statements were just too obvious! But I began to ask myself: If the sheikh's simple claims were indeed so self-evidently true and valid, why is it that Christians who are doctors, engineers, and university professors still believe in the Holy Trinity? Was I missing something? Frustrated, I concluded that if I wanted to find out what Christians really believed, I would need to listen to Christians themselves, not Muslims talking about Christianity.

Here I decided to change my approach, and I thought I might find help from Christians in my own neighborhood. As I mentioned above, the Christians in my area were all afraid to talk to me, and this posed was a major obstacle to communication. By this time, everyone thought I was either working for security or trying to convert them to Islam. One of the Christians refused to speak to me or even to give me a Bible! He said I cannot give it to you by hand, or the authorities may arrest me. Instead, I was sent a URL link to the Bible. So, I accessed the Bible first on my computer. Soon, I found myself reading the Gospel of John: "In the beginning was the Word, and the Word was with God, and the Word was God. He was at the beginning with God."

I was perplexed. Was this philosophy or English literature like Charles Dickens? I understood nothing. All these verses were about Jesus, not God! There was no mention of Allah? Where were Allah's commandments? I was expecting to read a Quranic Bible, as I understood the Quran to be the template and model for any holy book from Allah.

I decided to search the internet to explore the defining doctrines of Christianity. I started to watch Ahmed Deedat debates, and again I became confused. When I watched Deedat debate Swedish pastor Stanley Sjöberg, I felt that Ahmed Deedat was right. However, when I watched his debate with Josh McDowell, I concluded that Ahmed Deedat knew nothing about Christianity. So, I struggled to acquire a reliable impression of true Christianity, until one day when something took me by surprise! I was surfing the internet, searching for a clue about Christianity. Suddenly, a window popped up on my computer screen with the question, "Do You Love Allah?" I thought it was a Muslim website because the name Allah is mainly used by Muslims. But, I soon discovered that the site it led to was Christian. It was a beautiful—but confusing—Christian website which covered the Bible from Adam to Jesus. It contained information about how Adam fell and how, through his disobedience, we lost all the glory and the presence of the LORD. It detailed how God had promised Adam and Eve that He would send a savior and that this savior would come from a woman's womb with no human male involved (Was that a foretelling of Jesus' virgin birth, I wondered?). It told of how Abraham had gone to sacrifice Isaac at God's direction, and how God redeemed the boy with a ram to sacrifice in his place, which he Himself provided. It explored how Jesus is the answer for all things. It claimed that Jesus is the sacrifice, the tabernacle, Moses' rock in the desert, and the one who pleased God more than anyone, and who remained sinless.

The website also provided questions for non-Christians to consider. For instance, how could 'Imran, the father of Mary, the sister of Moses and Aaron, be the father of Mary the mother of Jesus —as the Quran claims? And since it was obviously not true, how could Allah allow His book to become corrupted in this way, allowing such basic factual flaws to creep into the Quran, which was supposedly His perfect and final word to humankind? Why did Allah not protect his word, the Quran? Such questions as these were new to me, because Muslims are not taught to question—certainly not the Quran, at least. We were told what to believe and were taught that it may harm us to ask questions, as the Quran taught (for example, Quran 5:101: "O you who believe! Ask not about things, which if revealed to you, would trouble you ...").

On the other hand, the website revived old questions that had occurred to me in the past, to which I had never received satisfactory answers. For instance, as a Muslim, I had wondered why Jesus had been endowed with such divine powers to heal, raise people from the dead and to give life. Yet, he is human, and divine at the same time! This was so confusing and incomprehensible to me. The Quran says the following about Jesus:

> And he will be a Messenger to the Children of Israel. (And when he came to them he said): "I have come to you with a sign from your Lord. I will make for you from clay the likeness of a bird and then I will breathe into it and by the leave of Allah it will become a bird. I will also heal the blind and the leper, and by the leave of Allah bring the dead to life. I will also inform you of what things you eat and what you treasure up in your houses." Surely this is a sign for you if you are true believers.[1]

Even according to Islam, Jesus possessed supernatural powers, such as creating living birds from mud, and the power of healing, which only God can do! As such, I began to doubt that could have been a mere prophet, since he was so distinguished from other prophets by these superhuman qualities. Even assuming he was only a prophet, why did God give these powers exclusively to Jesus, and not to other prophets?

When I used to ask Muslim scholars these questions, the answer I received from them was that Jesus performed all these miracles, "by permission of Allah." So, it was not Jesus's power; it was God's power.

I never agreed with this line of thinking, because power, which Jesus clearly possessed exclusively, is different from permission. If, as a building planner, I gave permission for a one-hundred-storey building to be erected, the applicant would still need the ability or power to erect the building. I would have given them the permission but not the power, which has to come from another source. So, the relevant question emerges again: Why was Jesus endowed with power which the Quran itself ascribes exclusively to God? As the Quran says "That is Allah your Rabb (Sustainer)! There is no god but Him, the Creator of everything. Therefore, worship Him, He is the Guardian of everything"[2] Based on such verses, I began to suspect that if God were the creator of everything, and Jesus has created birds, then perhaps Jesus is God! Elsewhere, the Quran says, "And if you speak aloud - then indeed, He knows the secret and what is [even] more hidden"[3] This verse should probably add that Jesus too knows secrets. These burning questions had been swirling in my head for years, and for years I sought answers from Muslim scholars, in vain.

Such issues caused me, for the first time in my life, to doubt my Muslim faith. I began to think, "Maybe we are wrong." That was a serious thought for someone like myself to entertain. I kept searching through my library and books, wondering how all these books could be wrong. Where they just full of hollow words? Could *Fatḥ al-Bārī fī Sharḥ Saḥīḥ al-Bukhārī*,[4] with all of its fourteen volumes, be empty words? Were *Sunan ibn Abī Dāūd, Minhaj al-Muslim, Tahzīb Minhaj al-Sālikīn, Riyādh aṣ-Ṣāliḥīn, Matn al-Shaṭbiah, Tafsīr al Qur'ān al-'azīm li-bn Kathīr,* and *Asbāb an-Nuzūl li-l Nisabūri* empty words? Were all these books useless jingles? Did every one of these sources of knowledge which had occupied my hungry mind for years have anything at all to do with the only true God? I struggled with such doubts, which now caused me tremendous distress. I was so emotionally numbed that I was even unable to cry despite the great sadness that these doubts had caused me. Had my Salafi friends been able to read my private thoughts, they would have accused me of apostasy right then and there.

Notwithstanding, I read that Christian website several times because I enjoyed it. I liked two things, in particular, about it. First, it managed to join the dots of the story on humankind. God is obviously behind all the scenes, from Adam and Eve, to Seth, Noah, Abraham, and David all the way until John the Baptist. Like a compass, all these scenes pointed to one person: Jesus Christ. In all these scenes, God—because of His great love for humankind—was executing His plan for the salvation of humanity.

This idea of the great plan of salvation was novel to me. I was struck by the revelation that we who have been entrapped in the snare of the devil, cannot free ourselves of its grip. We are incapable of saving ourselves, and need a savior who is none other than Jesus Christ, the One who came to release us from the snares of Satan.

Second, everything was detailed on the website; it clearly told who did things, and where, when, and why. By contrast, the Quran's narrative is almost totally bereft of temporal or geographical context. In the Quran, the stories of the prophets are isolated, disjointed and not harmonized with other prophets or linked in any pattern. By comparison, the Bible provides plausible, rational and comprehensible details—and these all testify to the Bible's authenticity. I considered the following verse:

> In the days of Herod, king of Judea, there was a priest named Zechariah, of the division of Abijah. And he had a wife from the daughters of Aaron, and her name was Elizabeth. And they were both righteous before God, walking blamelessly in all the commandments and statutes of the Lord. But they had no child, because Elizabeth was barren, and both were advanced in years. (Luke 1:5-7)

The wealth of context in one verse includes:

1. In the time of a king Herod
2. King of Judea
3. Priest name Zechariah
4. From the division of Abijah
5. He had a wife
6. She is from the line of Aaron
7. Her name was Elizabeth

Seven factual details from one single verse! This was really amazing and new to me. I could not help noticing the sharp contrast with the Quran; I considered, in comparison, the following ayat (verse) from Surat Yā'-Sīn (verses 13-17):

> And present to them an example: the people of the city, when the messengers came to it. When We sent to them two but they denied them, so We strengthened them with a third, and they said, "Indeed, we are messengers to you." They said, "You are not but human beings like us, and the Most Merciful has not revealed a thing. You are only telling lies." They said, "Our Lord knows that we are messengers to you, and we are not responsible except for clear notification."

When held alongside biblical passages like the one quoted before, the total absence of basic contextual details in the Quran is astonishing. What was the event or occasion? In which city did this event (whatever it was) take place? Who were the messengers? They were three messengers, but who were they? Who disagreed with them? And why? When did this (whatever it was) take place? The Quran provides no answers. One might hope to gain some help by reading Muslim commentaries and exegeses, but most of these contradict one another and are clearly based on assumptions, lacking any reliable basis.

In the coming days, I felt compelled to visit and revisit that website. My doubt regarding the authenticity of the Quran and the truthfulness of the Muslim faith grew stronger every time I looked at it. It dealt with so many of the questions which had troubled me, that I had never dared to voice. For instance, what is the evidence that Islam is true? How did Allah fail to protect all his holy books? How can an infinite Allah be sitting on a finite throne? Does this not limit a limitless divinity? If Allah has actually predetermined everything, why would He judge me? Why should I be held responsible for deeds and events out of my control, because Allah controls everything? After a few days, with no answers to my questions, and filled with a raging inner tempest of confusion, I felt as if my head was going to explode. Have I been deceived all these years? Why was I never allowed to explore these questions?

At this point, I lost my faith in Islam. I lost my faith in any god, for that matter. I became an atheist. If the god of Islam did not exist, then no other God could exist.

Although the website was somewhat convincing, I was afraid to follow the path to which it was pointing, for fear of trying something new. I was not ready for a new journey of faith. My mind was filled with doubts. I started even to question my own existence. Perhaps my whole life was a nightmare from which I will wake up soon.

---

1. Surat Ali ʿImrān (Quran chapter 3), verse 49
2. Surat al-Anʿām (Quran chapter 6), verse 102. See also, an-Naḥl (Quran chapter 16), verses 17-20. Also, al-Hajj (Quran chapter 22), verse 73.
3. Surat Taha (Quran chapter 20), verse 7
4. The most well-known respected book for Sunni Muslims after the Quran itself

5

HOW NOTHING CREATED EVERYTHING

DNA neither cares nor knows. DNA just is. And we dance to its music.

— RICHARD DAWKINS, *RIVER OUT OF EDEN: A DARWINIAN VIEW OF LIFE*

Becoming an atheist marked a new season in my life. I entered it secretly, knowing that I could not share my true spiritual state with anyone. Meanwhile, I felt obliged to continue business as normal. I had to go to the mosque, pray with people, lead them in prayer, and fast in front of others ... but I did not do any of these things when I was alone. By merely pretending to be a Muslim, rather than actually being one, I put my own life in danger, since in Islam apostasy is punishable by death. I was placing my family in a difficult position, for if they learned that I had left Islam and became an apostate—*murtad*, as we say in Arabic—they would feel greatly embarrassed, and their loyalty would be torn between me and the Muslim community.

My apostasy caused me a tremendous amount of stress. I used to put on my jilbab—Muslim mens' distinct clothing—and on my way to prayer at the mosque I used to ply myself with what seemed like a thousand questions. With every step, I wondered, "What am I doing?" I contemplated killing myself and putting an end to this miserable life. In the end, I decided not to because there were a lot of things that I wanted to do before dying.

So, I began to have a secret life that nobody knew about, full of sin. After I decided that no God existed, I became eager to do everything that had been forbidden. I resolved that my fear of God was the only barrier between me and the sinful things that I otherwise would want to do. If there were no God, this meant that I could do whatever I wanted. Using a pretended concern for security as a pretext, I trimmed my beard. I began to do drugs like hash, acid, and marijuana. I committed adultery and got involved in other immoral relationships. People who were close to me came to know that I was a prayer leader in the morning and a perverted person at night. Because of this, they called me "Satan." I actually liked the label, as it gave me a feeling of freedom from religion and represented a stance against religion. At that time, I wanted to take revenge against Islam, because this religion had deceived me and made me look like a fool for my whole life. I was not happy to lose God, but I was pleased to gain my freedom, or at least what I thought to be my freedom.

Although a double life became the norm for me, it distressed and exhausted me psychologically and spiritually. I thought that sin would set me free. But in reality, it made enslaved me to sinning. I even started to use my skills to persuade others to live in sin. For example, if anyone sat with me for five minutes, I could convince them that there is nothing more worthwhile in life than hash, and that we cannot be sure if there were someone 'up there' to judge us. I would not say that I was spreading atheism, but I really wanted everyone to be set free from the idea of Islam, and this was my way of fulfilling that aim. People cannot easily resist pleasure and that is why it was not difficult for me to lead people into sin. My approach was very easy: I would state simply, "What is wrong with having fun?" "What is wrong with being high, as long as you know how to control yourself?" "Would God be really upset just because you are happy?" And so forth. And people fell for that. I found that many people actually wanted someone to validate their sin. They so badly wanted to commit sin, but they needed someone to open the door to pleasure for them and ease their troubled consciences.

Meanwhile, though, I myself became more enslaved to sin than ever before. I knew in my heart that I was doing wrong. I felt like a hypocrite and did not know what to do or how to get out of it. I tried to study atheism to support my ideas, but the more I learned about atheism, the more I felt confused, as it seemed that atheism required more faith than theism did. I *needed* to believe that there is "nothing" except some universe which came from nothing, and is led by nothing, without any point or purpose. I needed also to believe that there is no meaning to life, and especially that my own life had no meaning! Although such sentiments carried me along at the time, they stood at loggerheads with what I knew in my heart to be true—for instance, that there is definitely meaning in saving a person who is dying and giving them life.

I spent many a day sitting at my window, sipping coffee and pondering over one question: "Why?!" That is, how can there be an existence without a purpose? Why does love exist? Why care? Happiness? Sadness? How can all these feelings be only a chemical reaction?! It couldn't be! I could not refute the claim of nothingness or purposelessness, but still, I could not digest the idea that there is nothing and we are just conforming to instructions coded on our DNA, as Richard Dawkins insisted to be the case. For example, what if my DNA wants to kill you? What prevents me from doing it? What if my freedom clashes with your freedom or what if my happiness is achieved by taking your life? Should I listen to such ideas? Or, can I oppose and resist? Yes, I can, because I am a moral being. But the question is, where did we get morals and moral values in the first place? The question is not merely about how we learned these values. It is about their origin or fountainhead. If there is no God, there simply can be no objective morality.

I mused over David Hume's belief that we are nothing but animals, yet I have never seen a group of monkeys in a meeting discussing social justice or monkey rights! I have never heard of monkeys organizing a campaign "Bananas for every monkey" or their launching a project to increase the yield of bananas for exportation to deprived monkeys around the world. I do not intend humor by these observations. But we, as human beings, must be more than just animals.

So, I began to doubt atheism. Contrary to what I had previously supposed, I knew that I was far from being free. I now found myself hopelessly enslaved to sin. I could tell that I was simply seeking to satisfy my desires and meet what I considered to be my needs, at any price and by any means. I started to put all these questions together, and I summarized them into seven main statements, statements that I expect might be of some help to other seeking atheists. I now could not believe in atheism because:

1. I couldn't believe that "nothing" created everything.
2. I couldn't believe life had no purpose other than enjoying the moment or slavishly expressing the instructions in my DNA.
3. I couldn't believe there was no good or bad—as would be required if a moral law does exist.
4. I couldn't believe, when looking at two paintings sharing many features, that one of them spontaneously evolved into another. I found it more credible to assume that they were both created—by the same artist.
5. If theism is a mere solution for people who are afraid of darkness, then how is atheism not (by logical contrast) a mere solution for people fearful of the light?
6. I couldn't believe that atheism furnished an adequate alternative to faith. I realized that it is just another system of belief, nothing more.
7. I couldn't accept that science contradicts faith, because ultimately science is a journey of discovering nature, while religion considers questions of purpose behind nature and the reason for its existence that science is powerless to answer.

All these were adequate reasons for me to doubt the validity of atheism. But the problem was that I did not know where to find the truth. I was certain that neither Islam nor atheism contained the truth. But if it was not to be found in those belief systems, how could I find the truth, and where could I look for it? Admittedly, deep inside me, I did indeed believe that God existed, but I was simply pretending that He did not. This confusion left me with a dilemma that pushed me toward one idea that I thought would satisfy my conscience: agnosticism.

I found that I did not know if answers to my questions even existed or could be found. "Maybe," I reasoned, "the words, 'Who knows?' could be enough to give my life meaning." I assuaged myself with a vague notion that God, if He existed, was too great to get to know. In many ways, I was still thinking like a Muslim, except that I now had no religious faith in my heart.

This period of my life was confusing. I really lacked a sense of purpose. What were human beings doing on earth? Why do we live, and how do we live? Where are we going after death? Where did we come from? I had no clue! But, at the same time, such questions, left unasked or unanswered, leave a life empty. And such questions repeated again and again in my mind, refusing to just vanish without reasonable answers. Why we are here? How can one plan a future without understanding the past and present?

Plagued by such basic questions that would not leave me alone, my life became like Hell on earth. The pointlessness of life virtually prevented me from doing anything. On a more positive side, I began to ponder rather pragmatically which makes life more purposeful, atheism or theism? I found it impossible to remain agnostic for long. Sooner or later, I believe, one's heart and mind begin to lean toward either atheism or theism. On the other hand, if God exists, His existence raises a major question: Why does this God not communicate with humankind? Or, does He? Does he lack social skills? If God does exist and if He is good, then surely He would want to communicate. And if He is omnipotent, then He would be *able* to communicate. If He is omnipresent, then it would be easy for him to communicate to any sentient creature as He wished. If He were truly wise, then He should know *how* to communicate! At any rate, such were some of my thought processes.

One day, while reading a book in my room about management, I was struck by something in a chapter about decision-making skills, and I felt that maybe this was exactly what I lacked! Well, I either lacked the skills to make a decision, or I was afraid of making a decision. At this point, I would have hated to lose my way or to feel deceived again, as I felt I had been deceived by Islam. I now formed the opinion that agnostic people didn't necessarily lack faith, but just "decision-making skills."

Accordingly, I felt it only right that I come off the fence and make a decision. I got pen and paper and set out to tabulate a level-headed comparison between atheism and theism. I rewrote the seven points that I had written before about atheism, and now added another five points about why I could also not remain an agnostic. I decided that I was not an agnostic because:

1. I was unable to ignore the subject of God's existence.
2. I could not see how adopting agnosticism solved my doubts about God. It simply postponed my having to deal with those doubts.
3. By nature, I am too decisive to be agnostic.
4. Agnosticism failed to provide an answer to the most important existential questions: origin, meaning, morality, and destiny.
5. I could not accept the uncertainty—demanded by agnosticism—regarding my own destiny after death.

Following this exercise, I concluded that the only rational conclusion is that God exists, though He may be detached and not involved in our lives. He has abandoned us? Maybe deism was the answer after all!

To be a deist is not popular in my country, where one may hear of atheists or agnostics. But one rarely encounters deism. I became a deist, however, because I was convinced that God existed, and that He can communicate with us, but because meanwhile I had also come to believe that He had rightly abandoned us because of our great evils. And, how could God be blamed for abandoning such a sinful human race? We do evil; we lead self-centered lives. We are too proud to seek God's help.

So, I became a deist and tried to reconcile myself to this new idea. All the while, I was still an imam (of sorts) by day, and a different person by night—not a "Satan" anymore, as I had ceased actively working to pervert people or persuade them to commit sin. I felt as though I had nothing to lose, for without true faith in a living and loving God, one possesses nothing and therefore can lose nothing. As such, I myself now lost all hope.

After all, what is the point of striving to be a better person if there is no possibility of knowing the answers to life's biggest questions? At the same time, deism provided at least a partial answer to some of these questions, such as all the evil that happens all around us, as well as all the suffering and pain.

So, I lived during this period as though I were a prodigal son who works in order to just barely survive. I really did not care about life, and that was tough. To make matters worse, I started to have a lot of relationship problems with my family and friends. Everything that could go wrong did go wrong. I carried an increasingly heavy burden in my heart. Life was became almost unbearable, and my tears became my companions every night. Drugs no longer helped me. Women were not enough to satisfy my deep spiritual hunger. I was desperate for true love which I craved with all my being. I hated my life, which was becoming more miserable than ever.

At the time, I was taking medication for anxiety and depression, one of which would occasionally cause me to hyperventilate to the point of fainting. That medication was a vasoconstrictor, and I was supposed to take only a single pill at night. Filled with hopelessness, however, one night I decided to take all my pills at once. What followed was so painful that I felt my blood vessels would explode. It would have been a horrible way to commit suicide.

For the first time since I began my journey searching for God, I realized that I had been wasting my life, this *precious* life. I started to think that the God of Islam was now punishing me for leaving Islam.

Or perhaps the true God, whoever He was, was punishing me for even trying to get to know Him. I didn't know. These and other thoughts swirled in my head. Every notion and its opposite! I wanted to die, but not with pain. I wanted to live, but not with sorrow and bitterness. In desperation, I cried out, "Dear God, if I die, I would be sorry for having failed to find you. If I survive, I vow to find the truth and worship you."

After two hours, the pain began to subside until it vanished completely. I was left exhausted, and I went to sleep immediately. The next day, I thought the whole day about what had just occurred and how life is unbearable in this way. I returned to God that night and I fell on my knees. I told him I could not take it anymore; I was about to kill myself. I earnestly begged God to do something! I cried a lot. I begged Him to somehow reveal Himself to me, for I could no longer bear my current situation. I cried until I was exhausted and fell asleep.

And that very night, I had an unusual dream!

6

A MAN AT THE DOOR

And I have other sheep that are not of this fold. I must bring them also, and they will listen to my voice. So, there will be one flock, one shepherd.

— JOHN 10: 16

As a rational person, I never really had much time for dreams and what they stood for. However, this dream was radically different. It was authentic. In it, I saw myself running down a very long road, shrouded in darkness with thorny tree branches, resembling the arms of an octopus. These were chasing me and trying to kill me. However, I could see a brightly-lit building at the end of the road, whose door was opened. In front of the door stood a man who shone gloriously, and who looked toward me. As I ran, I begged him for help, "The tree branches are going to kill me; please do something!" He stretched his arm and reached out to me; his hand was frightfully enormous. I would be crushed by it! To my relief, his hand was so tender when he put it on my shoulder and immediately drew me to himself. At that very moment, everything stood still. He looked deep into my eyes.

This man looked familiar, as if I had seen him before, perhaps in pictures. Later, I realized it was Jesus Christ. His gaze penetrated deep into my heart, and He said: "*It is your time to follow me.*" I woke up immediately. It had been an astonishing dream, and I told myself that it was undoubtedly a hallucination.

The dream, however, preoccupied me for the entire day. Why this dream? Why me? Strangely, I experienced the same dream again the following night. At this point, I became angry, as I was puzzled and confused by these dreams. What relationship did these dreams bear to reality? Have I really seen and heard Jesus Christ? I looked out of the window and contemplated doing something out of the ordinary for a Muslim: I decided to challenge God! I looked at the sky and said, "If you are really Jesus, come to me once more with the exact details." Now, I did not expect Jesus to come to me. I knew that God does not like challenges from His creatures who should know their place far beneath Him. I knew that those who challenge Him are destined for Hell. What on earth had I done?! I slept that night and was almost sure that He would not come again.

But to my amazement, He came!

This time He said to me: "*Didn't I tell you: It is your time to follow me?*" I woke up surprised, crying in fear. I never believed that He would revisit me. More importantly, His presence brought a huge sense of embracing love into my room. That Jesus Christ could be that loving was a completely new revelation to me. His love, which I felt in the dream, covered me like a flood. I had never experienced such love in my life. I had rejected Him, yet he still came to me, which told me that I mattered a lot to Him.

Although upon waking up I was not a convert to Christianity, I was deeply fascinated by Jesus Christ and I determined to know more about who He really was. Who is this man about whom I had read on that website and who now had come to me personally— three times—in a dream?

The first idea which occurred to me was to access the Gospel of John on my computer. I read it once more. "In the beginning was the Word, and the Word was with God, and the Word was God. He was in the beginning with God. All things were made through him, and without him was not any thing made that was made." This time, I somehow understood: This is Jesus! The truth had finally dawned on me. At last, I began to understand who Jesus is.

There now followed a three-year long journey of discovery, during which I searched through both Muslim and Christian scriptures. Why Muslim scripture? Because, hitherto, Muslim scripture had been my only source of knowledge about God. As such, for whatever reason I felt at the time that I needed to study it in order to try to understand what had been going on in my life. And, my mind needed to be satisfied as I pondered these questions about the man I had encountered in my dream.

The first two points in my research were focused on the crucifixion of Jesus Christ and the authenticity of the Quran and the Bible. Why these two subjects? Because Jesus' crucifixion is a point of serious disagreement between Muslims and Christians. Secondly, if we are to trust the doctrines of either faith, we ought to first establish the authenticity of the scriptures on which these two faiths are based. So, I started by searching the evidence for the Quran. This time, however, I was not searching as a Muslim who swallows everything because he is desperate for Islam to be correct, but rather as an outsider earnestly seeking to know the simple and pure truth.

Jesus' Crucifixion

With this new, more honest mindset, what I found out about Jesus' crucifixion in Islam was very strange, so much so that I now wondered how I ever used to believe it! The simplistic answer given by Islam is that Jesus had not been crucified, as the Quran says in Surah an-Nisā' (Quran chapter 4), verse 157,

> And because of their saying (in boast), "We killed Messiah 'Isa (Jesus), son of Maryam (Mary), the Messenger of Allah," but they killed him not, nor crucified him, but the resemblance of 'Isa (Jesus) was put over another man (and they killed that man), and those who differ therein are full of doubts. They have no (certain) knowledge; they follow nothing but conjecture. For surely, they killed him not [i.e., 'Isa (Jesus), son of Maryam (Mary)]

The very strange thing, I now realized, is that while the Quran denies the crucifixion of Jesus, nowhere does Islam provide a plausible and trustworthy alternate narrative. Islam does not tell us *who* was crucified in place of Jesus. Nor does it explain *how* such a mistaken identity could have played out. Therefore, Muslim commentaries are full of conflicting accounts concerning what actually happened.

Ibn Kathīr and aṭ-Ṭabari provide the following explanation of how Jesus escaped crucifixion:

- Some said: We don't know
- And some said: All the disciples turned into the image of Jesus.
- And some said: A young man among them (who resembled Jesus), and in the same hadith the disciples divided into three groups: the Jacobites: they said God was among us and then ascended...and the Nestorians: they said that the Son of God was among us and then ascended...and the Muslims: they said he was the servant of God and His Messenger.
- And some said: Someone with the name Sarges, by treason
- And some say: Someone with the name Youdes Zacharias Youta, by treason

On the same question, here is the interpretation of al-Qurtubi:

And it was said: They differed in that the Nestorian Christians said: Jesus was crucified in the flesh, but his divinity was untouched. The Melkites said: The death and crucifixion of Christ occurred completely to both his humanity and divinity. They differed further and said: If the crucified person was one of the disciples, where is Jesus? And if it was Jesus who was crucified, where is the disciple?! It was also said that they differed in that the Jews said: We killed him. Because Judas, the head of the Jews, had sought to kill him. Another denomination of Christians said: It was we who killed him.

Another Christian denomination said: Rather, God raised him to heaven while we were looking at him.[1]

One major problem is that these groups of people mentioned by al-Qurtubi, not to mention the un-named "some" referenced by Ibn Kathīr and aṭ-Ṭabari, were not contemporaries of Jesus at all, but were born a long time after his ascension would have occurred. Nor did these exegetes have access to any eyewitnesses. In addition, Jesus' crucifixion can be said to be historical in that it is attested to, not only by eyewitnesses as recorded in the New Testament, but also by external (Roman, Greek, and even Jewish) sources. Following is a partial list.

Historians

Cornelius Tacitus[2] lived from 56 to 117 AD, and was one of the greatest Roman historians and authors, renowned for his accuracy and integrity. He was called the great historian of Rome. His life extended through six imperial reigns. One of his most famous books was the Annals and Histories, which contains many references to Christ and Christianity.

One of Tacitus' documents clearly states that Christianity derived its name from Christ and that Pontius Pilate was the one who sentenced him to death. As for the "myth" or "rumor" (Tacitus was not a Christian) alluded to in this document, it is undoubtedly the Resurrection.

Pliny the Younger[3] lived from 61 to 112 AD, and was governor of the province of Pontus. He wrote to Emperor Trajan about the death of Christians who rejected imperial worship because they followed and worshipped Jesus Christ.

Gaius Suetonius Tranquilias[4] lived from 69 to 140 AD, and was chief clerk to the Roman emperor Hadrian (117 to 138 AD). His job allowed him to view the official state records, and he referred to the reasons that led to the persecution of Christians, amongst which was their belief in the crucifixion, death, and resurrection of Christ. He did not deny the truth of these events.

Thallus the Historian died in the year 52 AD and is one of the great historians of the Rome, who wrote a history of the nations of the eastern Mediterranean from the Trojan War up until his own time. Although his actual writings have been lost, they have survived in the form of quotations contained in many history books, including those written by the historian Julius Africanus (the African), one of the historians who lived in the year 221 AD and was then martyred. Julius quotes from Thallus' history concerning the great darkness that fell upon the land when Jesus was crucified.

In the third volume of his history, Thallus tries to provide an alternative explanation for the darkness associated with the crucifixion as an eclipse of the sun, which in itself is remarkable, if true.

Julius the African rejected this reasoning (in 221 AD), basing his opinion on a scientific fact that a complete eclipse cannot occur during the full moon. "The time of the Passover celebration is when the moon is complete." The darkness and accompanying events were mentioned by Thallus in the third volume of his series of historical books:

> Darkness covered the whole world, and an earthquake cracked the rocks, and many places in Judea and other regions were cast down and destroyed by the earthquake.[5]

This quotation seems to confirm that unusual—and possibly miraculous—phenomena did take place during the crucifixion of Christ, to the extent that they left an impression upon the souls of non-believers such as Thallus.

Thallus was not the only one who stressed the occurrence of this darkness. Many of the ancients, such as Philopon the astronomer in the second century, also referred to it when he wrote:

> Phlegon mentioned the eclipse which took place during the crucifixion of the Lord Jesus Christ, and no other (eclipse); it is clear that he did not know from his sources about any (similar) eclipse in previous times...and this is shown by the historical account of Tiberius Ceasar.[6]

Although not contemporaneous to the events, the incident was also acknowledged and referenced by Imam al-Ḥāfiz Ibn Kathīr, the fourteenth century Islamic historian, in his book *al-Bidāya wa-l Nihāyah* ("The Beginning and the End"), Volume 1:182.

Dionysius the Areopagite, the judge.[7] From the first half of the first century AD, Dionysius was a pagan studying at Ain Shams University (one of the ancient Greek universities in Egypt, of course, different from Ain Shams University currently in Egypt!).

Dionysius was a student of astronomy, engineering, law, medicine, and other subjects—this was the approach of one who assumed the authority of judge, which is that he would become familiar with all the sciences. The learned Dionysius affirmed that the darkness had occurred, and initially offered three possibilities as to the meaning:

1. The world (at that time) was about to end, and this eclipse was one of the portents foretelling it.
2. All the rules of astronomy, including their basic rules, were mistaken.
3. The god of the universe was in pain.

The darkness at the crucifixion of Jesus remained impressed upon the memory of Dionysus until the Apostle Paul preached to him in the Areopagus, at which time he recalled the possibilities that he had studied and became convinced that the third one—i.e., that the God of the universe was in pain—was the most likely and correct of the three, because the event of darkness that occurred broke the rules of astronomy and scientific norms.

Now, one skeptical of the fact of the crucifixion of Christ may choose to overlook all the above evidences (and more to follow), in an attempt to evade the reality of the crucifixion story. He may, as many Muslims do, claim that someone other than Jesus was crucified, and that it was another person upon whom God placed the likeness of Christ. I believe, however, that the historical witnesses referenced above regarding the darkness that befell the earth at the time of the crucifixion, provides compelling evidence that the crucified person was God manifest in the flesh, as was claimed by the New Testament writers. Otherwise, this likeness would not have had the power to influence nature in such a monumental way. Anyone who wants to see the only path that leads to eternal life must first of all open the eyes of their mind. But some people have a blindfold the eyes of their mind and closed their hearts to the message of Christ. Such people will not understand the Gospel of Christ, and will be held responsible for their decision.

Lucian of Samosata[8] was one of the most prominent historians of Greece at the turn of the second century AD. He commented in a satirical critical article on Christians and Christ's crucifixion in the book "The Death of Bergernaut" to Lucian (born in 100 AD).

Phlegon of Tralles[9] was a second century pagan historian who wrote a history he called "Chronicles of the Days" that no longer exists except through other writers who have quoted him. Like Thallus, Phlegon confirms that darkness engulfed the earth at the time of Christ's crucifixion by saying, "During the reign of Tiberius Caesar, there was an eclipse of the sun at the time of the full moon."[10] Phlegon commented that such a thing had never happened before and repeats the detail that Dionysius (the Areopagite, first century) had cried out when he saw the darkness, saying, "Either the god of nature is in pain now, or the world is about to be destroyed." The darkness at that time, as mentioned earlier, was also referred to by the philosopher Tertullian[11] in the second century AD.

Jewish sources

The early Jewish sources are strongly anti-Christian, but even so, no Jewish source denied that the crucifixion of Jesus, called the Christ, had occurred.

Flavius Josephus was an acclaimed Jewish historian (37 to 97 or 100 AD). His book, *The Dates*, written between the years 90-95 AD, contains a paragraph on the crucifixion of Christ.[12] Josephus also wrote of James, who he says was the brother of a Jesus who claimed to be the Messiah.[13] The testimony of Josephus, therefore, preceded the records of the majority of pagan historians listed above. When we consider that Josephus was famous among his peers for objectivity and that he dealt with this historical incident through Jewish records, it becomes difficult to deny that this text is reliable and worthy of trust.

Mara bar Serapion, born around year 50, was a Syriac Stoic philosopher in the Roman province of Syria. He is only known from a letter he wrote in Syriac to his son, who was named Serapion, which refers to the execution of "the wise king of the Jews" and may be an early non-Christian reference to Jesus of Nazareth.[14]

The *Jewish Talmud* is divided into two main groups: the Mishna and the Gemara. The former is the ancient oral tradition inherited by successive generations of the Jewish community and then written down in the second century AD. The Gemara, is a collection of explanations, discussions, disputations, and commentaries on the Mishna. Many different religious and legal opinions are contained in the Talmud, so just because a statement appears inside it does not mean that the statement is true or endorsed by Judaism. It is, rather, part of the discussion among religious authorities. However, what concerns us it the appearance of historical reports concerning Jesus death. And, the Talmud does contain the following statement:

> On the eve of the Passover, Yeshu was hanged. For forty days before the execution took place, a herald cried, "He is going forth to be stoned because he has practiced sorcery and enticed Israel to apostasy. Anyone who can say anything in his favor, let him come forward and plead on his behalf." But since nothing was brought forward in his favor, he was hanged on the eve of the Passover.[15]

Toledot Yeshu, a medieval (that is, not early) Jewish manuscript that is stridently anti-Christian, accuses Jesus of being an illegitimate son and describes him as a sorcerer. It accepts the premise that Jesus was crucified and alleges that the practice of sorcery was the reason he died dishonorably by crucifixion.[16]

Having found so many attestations of the crucifixion of Jesus, even through his mockers and haters, I could, by this stage, confidently say that Jesus had definitely been crucified. Sadly, of the three

Semitic faiths, Islam is the only one which denies Jesus' evident and well attested crucifixion. I could see that the Muslim position *vis-à-vis* the crucifixion of Christ, if not so tragic, would be hilarious; it accuses God of—on the one hand—having deceived people, and—on the other hand—of having punished an innocent man.

When I share my testimony, many people ask me, how, as an ex-Muslim, I dealt with the Trinity and the incarnation of God? In response, I usually make two points: the first is that I have always believed that God can do whatever He wants, including being incarnate in human flesh. Why would such a feat be difficult for an omnipotent God? As for the Trinity, I saw that God is different from humans, and that He is who He is. If God is eternal, existing from the beginning, and if God is love, whom did He love at the beginning, when there was not yet a creation? The answer is that He loved the Son and the Holy Spirit who also loved each other and Him. The three persons of the Godhead loved one another. Without this mysterious detail, God's love would be rendered a hollow—non-eternal—attribute. Love must have an object. The one being we call Yahweh, shared his love internally among his three Persons. Even though I only gradually grasped its importance, the way the Trinity settles this problem proved deeply satisfying to my mind.

Years later, I did my master's thesis on the subject of the Trinity, at which point I built upon these theological foundations.

Authenticity of the Bible and the Quran

The second important thing to consider was the question of the authenticity of the books. I began with the Bible, of course. And, if the Bible is true, then what it says about the Trinity (even if that *word* does not exist in its text) would also be true.

When I considered the Trinity, I found that it could be illustrated somehow in the letters:

The first Hebrew letter in the alphabet is א, and it is pronounced "*alef*." If I asked you, "How many letters is א in Hebrew?" most people would say, "One letter." But actually, it is אלף = *alef*, so even when it is three letters in Hebrew, no one would say that א is three letters; since alef is itself only one letter. So, א is one letter from its essence but it is three letters together from another sense.

Ultimately, no analogy will be sufficient because nothing can be like the Trinity, but this is one illustration for how I was able to understand that the concept of the Trinity of God is not nonsensical.

After studying for a while, I became convinced that the Christian faith is true, and I started searching for someone to teach me more about it. I found an answer to my need through the *Paltalk* phone application, where people from all over the world could go to discuss religion. Having used it before, when I was a Muslim, to debate and watch Christian Muslim discussions, it was easy for me to enter Christian chat rooms and hear what they were saying and teaching about Christianity. I found myself in one room, where one pastor was teaching about the authenticity of the Bible. It was precisely the subject I was searching for. As I paid attention, this pastor eventually taught me a lot about the greatness of the Bible, how Christianity has something called manuscripts, and that these manuscripts had been subjected to textual criticism. I was surprised to find that, unlike Muslims who are forbidden from even asking questions, Christians went so far as criticizing their own holy book! It dawned on me that, far from being an expression of disbelief, textual criticism revealed how confident Christians were of the authenticity of their holy book. By contrast, Muslims dare not question or evaluate their Quran, for fear of the truth, that is the Quran defies all logic and rules of authenticity. Therefore, early Muslim leaders imposed an ostrich approach towards their holy scripture.

The following facts left me feeling astounded:[17]

- Christians have 5858 manuscripts of the Greek New Testament (NT), amounting to a total of about 2.6 million pages.
- There are 233 NT manuscripts dating to the second and third centuries AD.
- There exist nearly twice as many Latin NT manuscripts as they have Greek NT manuscripts dating from the late second century until the fourth century AD.

- Christians have approximately 10,000 NT manuscripts written in languages other than Greek and Latin (the NT was always handwritten prior to the invention of the printing press).
- Altogether, Christians possess 24,000 to 25,000 manuscripts of the New Testament.
- In addition, there are over 1 million quotations by church fathers from the New Testament. The entirety of the Greek New Testaments contains, 7941 verses. This means that the early church fathers, disciples of the disciples of Jesus, and their disciples, quoted the New Testament extensively. As a result, we have almost the entire New Testament preserved in these secondary writings, and they do not differ significantly with the New Testament text Christians have today.

It is truly unfortunate that I had never heard of these vital facts before. But my exposure to these details removed all my doubts concerning the authenticity of the Bible and the Christian faith, and I now became certain that it is, rather, Islam and its scriptures that are inauthentic. But that is not the only reason I left Islam. I summarize my various other reasons for abandoning Islam below.

First, I couldn't believe that God can be just one person in one nature, because God is love. How could God be loving if He is just one person, on His own? What could love even *mean* in that situation? Whom did He love before creation? The general discussion of my reasoning on this matter follows. *Today, I perceive that the God of Islam is imperfect compared to the one true God of Christianity.*

1. God is the greatest conceivable being ever. Therefore, God should be perfect.
2. Love is the highest moral value we know. Therefore, God should be loving.
3. Love is a relationship in which one party gives to the other, not only inwardly-focused as a selfish being.

4. If God exists and has the attribute of being loving, *who is the other before anything was created*? The foundational object of God's attribute of being loving can't be any created thing; because creation is a result of God's free will, not a result of God's nature.

5. It follows that the other to whom God's love is necessarily directed, must somehow be internal to God himself.

6. Love within God can only exist if God is in some way plural and not a single, isolated person.

7. In Islam, God is focused upon Himself; He is not a person who gives himself away essentially in love for another. As such, the Islamic God could not be the most perfect being.

8. In Christianity, God is a triad of persons in eternal self-giving love relationship, a Tri-unity. This specialized compound word is shortened to *Trinity*.

9. It was not incumbent upon God to create anything if He did not want to do so. He was God before creation, and He could have chosen never to create anything. But he *must* be loving. Since a reality in which God never created anything is possible without violating His eternal attributes, the proposition of God existing without some internal plurality of person is simply untenable.

10. The Trinity, therefore, is not only rationally *acceptable* and *plausible*; it is *necessary*.

Second, I couldn't believe that the only proof of Muhammad's prophecy is the Quran, while the only evidence that the Quran is true is that Muhammad said so. In logic, such an argument is known as the "circular reasoning fallacy." It only looks strong to simple-minded people. Circular reasoning is completely empty.

Now, Muslims sometimes do present other arguments beyond the supposed miracle of the Quran itself to demonstrate that Muhammad was a prophet. For example, some claim that he actually did miracles, or that his behavior proves that he is a prophet. But these claims are inconsistent with the Quran itself, which states,

And nothing has prevented Us from sending signs except that the former peoples denied them. And We gave Thamud the she-camel as a visible sign, but they wronged her. And We send not the signs except as a warning.[18]

And they say, "Why has a sign not been sent down to him from his Lord?" Say, "Indeed, Allah is able to send down a sign, but most of them do not know."[19]

And those who disbelieved say, "Why has a sign not been sent down to him from his Lord?" You are only a warner, and for every people is a guide.[20]

And they say, "Why is a sign not sent down to him from his Lord?" So say, "The unseen is only for Allah [to administer], so wait; indeed, I am with you among those who wait."[21]

And is it not sufficient for them that We revealed to you the Book which is recited to them? Indeed, in that is a mercy and reminder for a people who believe."[22]

In the last verse, we see what seems to be the Quran's own clearest assertion that Allah sent only the Quran as a miracle.

And, there are other verses like those shown above. Even so, some Muslims say that we have different hadith that tell about Muhammad talking to a palm tree, or that stones praised God while he held them in his hand, but in my view these Hadith really show us only two things. First, they show that the Quran often contradicts the Hadith. And second, they show that we cannot trust many hadiths because they were written so many years after Muhammad. In fact, we have no contemporary record of eyewitness accounts for any of these incidents.

Another common statement by Muslims is, "But we have a verse in the Quran that proves Muhammad's miracles, Surat al-Qamar (Quran chapter 54), verse 1, 'The Hour has come near, and the moon has split [in two].'" Concerning such a statement, we can say two things. First, assuming we agree that the verse refers to an actual splitting of the moon during Muhammad's time and not (for example) about the end-times, then it is another example of contradiction inside the Quran. But the most important detail to me is, second, what happened when a man who assumed the former scenario sent the National Aeronautics and Space Administration (NASA) a question:

> This website: https://www.mastikorner.com/forum/islamic-picx/ 6843-miracle-prophet-muhammad-p-b-u-h.html claims that Allah split the Moon in two at the request of the Prophet Muhammad and that there is a split on the Moon documented by American scientists that goes right around it which is evidence of the miracle. Is there any truth to any of these claims?

NASA responded as follows:

> My recommendation is to not believe everything you read on the internet. Peer-reviewed papers are the only scientifically valid sources of information out there. No current scientific evidence reports that the Moon was split into two (or more) parts and then reassembled at any point in the past. Brad Bailey, NLSI, Staff Scientist, June 21, 2010[23]

So, I could understand if these hadiths meant to speak metaphorically, but they do not work ontologically.

For those who will speak about Muhammad's behaviors and many of his good deeds—and not only his, but also those of his companions who supposedly protected his words and transmitted them to us—I would respond:

> The Muslims fought a total of twenty-nine battles during the life of the Prophet Muhammad, some of which were fought by Muhammad himself and some of which were led and/or participated in by Muhammad, which are listed below.

As Maulana Wahiduddin Khan, a contemporary Islamic scholar, says, "During the 23 years in which this revolution was completed, 80 military expeditions took place."

According to Ibn Isḥāq, Muhammad personally attended twenty-seven expeditions.[24] Not all of them were battles. In some cases, he never located his enemy. In others, the purpose was non-military. These twenty-seven were:

1. The raid of **Waddan** which was the raid of al-Abwa'
2. The raid of **Buwat** in the direction of Radwa
3. The raid of 'Ushayra in the valley of Yanbu'
4. The **first** fight at **Badr** in pursuit of Kurz ibn Jabir
5. The **great** battle of **Badr** in which God slew the chiefs of the Quraysh and their nobles and captured many
6. The raid on the Banu Sulaym until he reached **al-Kudr**
7. The raid of **al-Sawiq** in pursuit of Abū Sufyān ibn Ḥarb until he reached Qarqara al-Kudr
8. The raid on the Ghatafan tribe toward Najd, which is the raid of **Dhu Amarr**
9. The raid of **Bahran**, a mine in the Hijaz above al-Furu'
10. The battle of **Uhud**
11. The raid of m**Hamra'u'l-Asad**
12. The siege of the **Nadir** tribe
13. The raid of **Dhatu'l-Riqa'** of Nakhl
14. The **non-battle** of **Badr**
15. The campaign against **Dumatu'l-Jandal**
16. The battle of the Ditch (**al-Khandaq**)
17. The siege of the **Qurayza** tribe
18. The expedition against the **Lihyan** of Hudhayl tribe
19. The raid of **Dhu Qarad**
20. The ambush of the **Mustaliq** of Khuza'a tribe at **al-Muraysi**
21. The expedition to **al-Hudaybiyya** (not intending to fight), where the polytheists opposed his passage (In fact, fighting did occur.)

22. The siege of **Khaybar**
23. The **minor pilgrimage** (non-military)
24. The conquest of **Mecca**
25. The ambush of **Hunayn**
26. The siege of **Ta'if**
27. The campaign to **Tabuk**

Then his successors led a lot of wars after Muhammad's death in 632:

- The *Ridda* ("Apostasy") wars, 632 AD, led by 'Abū Bakr, Muhammad's first successor
- The conquest of Persia, 633 AD
- The conquest of Damascus, 635 AD
- The conquest of Jerusalem, 638 AD
- The conquest of Egypt, 640 AD
- and others

These are the Quran's and Muhammad's orders concerning how to deal with non-Muslims:

The believers may not take the unbelievers for their allies in preference to those who believe. Whoever does this has nothing to do with Allah unless he does so in order to protect himself from their wrong-doing. Allah warns you to beware of Him for it is to Allah that you will return.[25]

Believers! Do not take the Jews and the Christians for your allies.[26] They are the allies of each other. And among you he who takes them for allies, shall be regarded as one of them. Allah does not guide the wrong-doers.[27]

Al-Bukharī said concerning Abū al-Darda': "We smile in the face of some people and our hearts curse them"[28]

I have been ordered (by Allah) to fight against the people until they testify that none has the right to be worshipped but Allah and that Muhammad is Allah's Messenger and offer the prayers perfectly and give the obligatory charity, so if they perform that, then they save their lives and property from me except for Islamic laws and then their reckoning (accounts) will be done by Allah.[29]

Abū Hurayra reported Allah's Messenger (that is, Muhammad) as saying: "Do not greet the Jews and the Christians before they greet you and when you meet any one of them on the roads force him to go to the narrowest part of it."[30]

Following is a translation of the Caliph ʿUmar's peace treaty with Ash-Sham (that is, Syria):

This is a document to the servant of Allah ʿUmar, the Commander of the Faithful, from the Christians of such and such city. "When you (Muslims) came to us we requested safety for ourselves, children, property and followers of our religion. We made a condition on ourselves that we will neither erect in our areas a monastery, church, or a sanctuary for a monk, nor restore any place of worship that needs restoration nor use any of them for the purpose of enmity against Muslims. We will not prevent any Muslim from resting in our churches whether they come by day or night, and we will open the doors (of our houses of worship) for the wayfarer and passerby. Those Muslims who come as guests will enjoy boarding and food for three days. We will not allow a spy against Muslims into our churches and homes or hide deceit (or betrayal) against Muslims. We will not teach our children the Quran, publicize practices of *shirk*,[31] invite anyone to *shirk* or prevent any of our fellows from embracing Islam, if they choose to do so. We will respect Muslims, move from the places we sit in if they choose to sit in them. We will not imitate their clothing, caps, turbans, sandals, hairstyles, speech, nicknames and title names, or ride on saddles, hang swords on the shoulders, collect weapons of any kind or carry these weapons. We will not encrypt our stamps in Arabic, or sell liquor. We will have the front of our hair cut, wear our customary clothes wherever we are, wear belts around our waist, refrain from erecting crosses on the outside of our churches and demonstrating them and our books in public in Muslim fairways and markets. We will not sound the bells in our churches, except discretely, or raise our voices while reciting our holy books inside our churches in the presence of Muslims, nor raise our voices (with prayer) at our funerals, or light torches in funeral processions in the fairways of Muslims, or their markets. We will not bury our dead next to Muslim dead, or buy servants who were captured by Muslims. We will be guides for Muslims and refrain from breaching their privacy in their homes." When I gave this document to 'Umar, he added to it, "We will not beat any Muslim. These are the conditions that we set against ourselves and followers of our religion in return for safety and protection. If we break any of these promises that we set for your benefit against ourselves, then our *dhimma*[32] is broken and you are allowed to do with us what you are allowed of people of defiance and rebellion."[33]

Third, I found it difficult to believe that the Quran would be protected or preserved by God, while the Injīl (i.e., the Gospel) and Torah (i.e., at least the five books of Moses), which the Quran freely concedes are God's Word, were *not* protected or preserved by God. Adding to my difficulty, the Quran has no reliable manuscripts, but the Injīl and Torah have. Moreover, as the Quran confirms, you cannot see any connection between God's words in different books.

Some others will try to leave the subject of Muhammad and instead give evidence that the Quran is the word of God that was never changed because has been fully preserved by God, word by word and letter by letter. They mostly use the verse,

Indeed, it is We who sent down the reminder [*adh-dhikr* (i.e., the Quran)] and indeed, We will be its guardian.[34]

Also, if we look elsewhere in the Quran, we find:

And We sent not before you except men to whom We revealed [Our Message]. So, ask the people of the Message if you do not know.[35]

Before this We wrote in the Psalms after the message (given to Moses): My servants the righteous shall inherit the earth.[36]

So, even if the verse in Surat al-Ḥijr (Quran chapter 15), verse 9—the first of three verses quoted above—talks about the Quran in this context, we must remember that Allah still has the Injīl, the Torah, and the Psalms, all of which are also His message and should be protected as well. We can see this detail quite clearly another verse,

He has sent down upon you, [O Muhammad], the Book in truth, confirming what was before it, and He revealed the Torah and the Gospel. Before, as guidance for the people. And He revealed the Quran. Indeed, those who disbelieve in the verses of Allah will have a severe punishment, and Allah is exalted in Might, the Owner of Retribution.[37]

Also, in another place the Quran says,

Nothing is said to you, [O Muhammad], except what was already said to the messengers. Indeed, your Lord is a possessor of forgiveness and a possessor before you of painful penalty.[38]

So, it is the same message and the same protection, supposedly, according to these verses. The question here, then, is, *If the Quran is protected word-for-word by God, why not the other books of revelation?*

The other problem here, is that the Quran was evidently not protected word by word at all, to the point that we need to ask, "Which Quran?"

Narrated Anas bin Malik: "Hudhaifa bin Al-Yaman came to ʿUthmān at the time when the people of Sham [i.e., Syria] and the people of Iraq were waging war to conquer Armenia and Azerbaijan. Hudhaifa was afraid of their (the people of Sham and Iraq)

differences in the (recitation) of the Quran, so he said to 'Uthmān, 'O chief of the Believers! Save this nation before they differ about the Book (Quran) as Jews and the Christians did before.' ... 'Uthmān sent to every Muslim province one copy of what they had copied, and ordered that all the other Quranic materials, whether written in fragmentary manuscripts or whole copies, be burnt."[39]

So, actually we will never be able to get many of the original manuscripts of the Quran—because 'Uthmān destroyed them!

Even Muhammad did not ask his people to keep the Quran, they were confused:

'Abū Bakr sent for me at a time when the Yamama battles had witnessed the martyrdom of numerous Companions. I found 'Umar bin al-Khattāb with him. 'Abū Bakr began, "'Umar has just come to me and said, 'In the Yamama battles, death has dealt most severely with the *qurra'* [reciters of the Quran] and I fear it will deal with them with equal severity in other theatres of war. As a result, much of the Quran will be gone.' I am therefore of the opinion that you should command the Quran be collected."

'Abū Bakr continued, "I said to 'Umar, 'How can we embark on what the Prophet never did?' 'Umar replied that it was a good deed regardless, and he did not cease replying to my scruples until Allah reconciled me to the undertaking, and I became of the same mind as him. ... [I said], 'Zayd, you are young and intelligent, you used to record the revelations for Muhammad, and we know nothing to your discredit. So, pursue the Quran and collect it together.' By Allah, had they asked me to move a mountain it could not have been weightier than what they requested of me now."[40]

What was Zayd ibn Thabit's comment after this request? He said,

...By Allah, if he ('Abū Bakr) had ordered me to shift one of the mountains it would not have been harder for me than what he had ordered me concerning the collection of the Quran... So, I started locating the Quranic material and collecting it from parchments, scapula, leaf stalks of date palms and from the memories of men.[41]

Zayd also said,

> So, I started looking for the Holy Quran and collected it from (what was written on) palm-leaf stalks, thin white stones, and also from men who knew it by heart, until I found the last verse of Surat at-Tawba (repentance) with Abi Khuzayma al-Ansārī, and I did not find it with anybody other than him.[42]

Also, there were several known versions of the Quran that had their own followings:

> The Islamic manuscript that ʿUthmān ibn Affān depended on, in collecting the Quran was one manuscript between several manuscripts which were used in the first four centuries of migration. They added: "There were other copies under the name of Muhammad's Companions that were popular in Kufa 'Ibn Massoud,' Basra 'Abi Mousa,' and Sham [i.e., Syria] 'Ubayy ibn Ka'b,' with many differences.[43]

They also referenced many books (around eleven) for high scholars that talk about differences of recitation, and even about different Qurans. For example, differences between the copies of Sham (i.e., Syria), Hijaz, and Iraq, according to Ibn Amir Alyahsebi, and there were also differences between the regional copies of Medina, Kufa, and Basra For Al Kasā'ī.

The popular book called *Kitāb al-Maṣāḥif* ("Book of the Copies") by Ibn Abī Dāūd, talked of around three thousand to nine thousand differences.

For example, also, Ibn Masʿūd was one of the close companions to Muhammad, it is narrated that he personally heard around seventy surahs directly from Muhammad. And, he was one of ten people who was promised heaven. Ibn Masʿūd was one of the people who wrote down the dictated message of the Quran from Muhammad. Also, he was an interpreter of the Quran in addition to serving as imam at the mosque and teaching the Quran text. Muhammad himself is reported to have said concerning Ibn Mas'ūd, "If you want to recite the Quran smoothly and tenderly, recite it the way of Ibn Um 'Abd (Ibn Mas'ūd)"

Ibn Mas'ūd's copy contained only **112 surahs,** because he did not accept the Quran's last two surahs[44] and he said they were only a prayer for Muhammad. Furthermore, he refused to accept 'Uthmān Ibn Affān's order to burn his own copy.

Other examples of differences include:

Examples of *different* surahs:

- In both the *muṣḥaf* of Ibn Abbās and *muṣḥaf* of Ubayy ibn Ka'b, there were surahs called Surah al-Khol'a and Surah al-Ḥifd.

Examples of *differences in verses*:

Surah An-Nisā' (Quran chapter 4) verse 24 in the standard Quran reads, "...So for whatever you enjoy {of marriage} from them, give them their due compensation as an obligation..."
However, Ibn Abbās read it, "...So for whatever you enjoy {of marriage} from them **to a definite period,** give them their due compensation as an obligation..."

Accordingly, we have twenty-eight copies besides the previous three main *muṣḥafs*.[45] So, according to the Sunni authorities, we have thirty-one *muṣḥafs* from before 'Uthmān burned all these copies.

Add to that the opinion of the Shia[46]:

1. One group says that they believe in it 100% and that it is guaranteed by God and all the narrated stories and opinions prove that it has no change or interpolation. They believe that the Quran was written during the time of Muhammad.

2. A second group says that it is correct *but not 100%,* as they can see some changes in almost two-thirds of the Quran and they believe that the Quran came from God with 17,000 verses, while the one we have now, has only 6,236 verses (just one-third the length of the original).

Muhammad Al Kulaynī, in his book *Al-Kāfī,* writes:

1. Example: Al-Mā'ida (Quran chapter 5), verse 67: "O Messenger, announce that which has been revealed to you from your Lord (**about Ali**), and if you do not, then you have not conveyed His message. And Allah will protect you from the people."
2. Kulaynī references a mushaf of Fatima
3. Ibn Hazm used to say: What the Shi'a say about the Quran is not an argument against Islam as they are not Muslims

Today also, we have the amazing research of Daniel Brubaker who by now has discovered and catalogued upwards of 4000 corrections (post-production alterations) in the earliest Quran manuscripts.[47]

In the end, we cannot ever be sure that we have one Quran as I have shown in addition to that what they call "Riwayat," or narrations of the Quran, but I do not want to go into this issue here, who knows, maybe in another book.

Fourth, and the Quran is impossible to comprehend without reference to the Sunnah and Tafsīr, where both are not protected even in the opinion of Islam.

Today, I have come to understand that the Quran is a book that lacks context to such an extent that tremendous portions of it cannot be anchored to details without reference to external sources. As I wrote above, there is often no indication of critical details such as "where," "when" or "who" without the commentaries and Hadith. One cannot tell the number of rak'ahs (kneeling[48]) merely by reading the Quran alone; one must look at the *sunnah* in order to know that. Also, one often cannot really say what the verses are talking about without *asbāb an-nuzūl* or "reasons of revelation," a category of secondary literature that purports to tell why, or in what situation, particular verses were revealed.

But the problem here is that these books of *sunnah* and commentaries were written by normal people who are not infallible and who did not claim to be prophets. Thus, we can have no assurance that they made no mistake in their judgments, especially considering that all these books were written a long time after Muhammad.

Muhammad lived from 570 A.D to 632 A.D

- Around 765 Ibn Isḥaq (Ṣirāt Rasūl Allah) (No extant manuscript)
- Around 833 Ibn Hisham (Ṣirāt Rasūl Allah)
- Around 870 Al-Bukhārī (Hadith), then *Saḥiḥ Muslim*, then Tirmidhi and others
- Around 923 Al Tabari (Tafsir, Tarikh), Baidawi, then Zamakshari and others.

As we see, none of these books have been written in the time of Muhammad or even close to the time of Muhammad. So how can we rely on all of these books as a source of knowledge, as if it is infallible while being unable to prove that it has no mistakes? One mistake is enough to bring it all under critique.

Fifth, I have found no evidence in Islam of God's unconditional universal love for His creatures. Allah only loves those who love him.

On the point of love, I have now come to believe that Islam has a morally deficient concept of God, because as they are agreed with Christianty on some basics such as God is all powerful, all knowing, and so on. However, He must also be all loving as a perfect being.

The Quran states quite clearly that Allah does not love those who do not obey Him. For example,

(O Messenger!) Tell people: "If you indeed love Allah, follow me, and Allah will love you and will forgive you your sins. Allah is All-Forgiving, All-Compassionate." Say: "Obey Allah and obey the

Messenger." If they turn away from this then know that Allah does not love those who refuse to obey Him and His Messenger."[49]

Not only that, but Allah loves specific people and hates others. According to the Quran, God *loves* those who

- do good (2:195, 3:146)
- are constantly repentant (2:222)
- purify themselves (2:222)
- fear Him (3:76)
- rely upon Him (3:159)
- act justly (5:42)
- love him (3:31)

Meanwhile, according to the Quran, God *hates*

- those who refuse to obey Him (3:32)
- those who disobey His Messenger (3:32)
- the unbelievers (30:45)
- the transgressors (2:190)
- every sinning disbeliever (2:276)
- the wrongdoers (3:57, 140)
- those who are self-deluding and boastful (4:36)

As you see, Allah's love is *conditional*. Given this statement, the central question becomes, "Who could have salvation if Allah hates him or her?" Another question becomew whether Allah is change-able if He may change his opinion about a person.

Sixth, I couldn't accept the self-contradictory claims of the Quran which was written for Arabs in their under-developed, archaic language, which most Muslims (regardless of their ethnicity) cannot read or understand, and yet it claims to be a message for all nations and for all time.

Today, I have come to believe that there are many rules in Islam that are not right. These include Islam's the laws of inheritance. Why, for example, are there some cases in which Islam insists upon giving a man double that given to a woman (Surat an-Nisā' (Quran chapter 4), verse 11)?

Other aspects that raise questions for me include rules concerning women covering their faces (e.g., wearing the hijab), as is instructed in Surat al-Ahzab (Quran chapter 33), verse 59, and the approval of the practice of taking and keeping sex slaves and other slaves (e.g., Surat an-Nisā' (Quran chapter 4), verse 36, and Surat al-Mu'minūn (Quran chapter 23), verses 5-6).

Not only that, we have big problem that the Quran is in one language:

1. If God can protect the book in one language, He can protect it in all languages.
2. Any language has a culture and development process that changes with time.
3. Insistence upon using the book in the Arabic language, even for those to whom the language is unknown and foreign, does not seem to align with the idea of an international message that is for all nations.

Arabic may not be the best language for preservation of a message, as it has many forms and poetic ways that would make it difficult to understand with precision what the author of the verses intends to say. Arabic in the first century of the Quran used silent letters [ie, without punctuation and disambiguating marks].[50]

These language limitations affected the meaning and the pronunciation of the Quran, and the issue was not fully resolved until the time of al-Hajjāj ibn Yūsuf in the period from 693 to 714 AD, that is, at least 74 to 95 years after the Hijra.[51] Al Hajjāj employed two persons to help with his Quran reforms, Naṣr ibn 'Āṣim al-Laythi, and Yahya ibn Ya'mor al-Adwānī. Being nearly a century after the death of Muhammad, there was a period of time, then, when some ambiguity existed in the written Quran manuscripts.

Here is one example of the problems for clarity that can arise in the Arabic if the dots distinguishing the letters from each other are absent.

> Surat al-Ahzab (Quran chapter 33), verse 53, *as it stands today:*

> O you who believe! Do not enter the houses of the Prophet except when you are permitted for a meal, without **awaiting its readiness**. But when you are invited, then enter; and when you have eaten, disperse without seeking to remain for conversation. Indeed, that [behavior] was troubling the Prophet, and he is shy of [dismissing] you. But Allah is not shy of the truth. *And when you ask [his wives] for something, ask them from behind a partition.* That is purer for your hearts and their hearts. And it is not [conceivable or lawful] for you to harm the Messenger of Allah or to marry his wives after him, ever. Indeed, that would be in the sight of Allah an enormity.

> The same verse *as it could have been read before the addition of dots:*

> O you who believe! Do not enter the houses of the Prophet except when you are permitted for a meal, without **looking at his wives** [ثينا]. But when you are invited, then enter; and when you have eaten, disperse without seeking to remain for conversation. Indeed, that [behavior] was troubling the Prophet, and he is shy of [dismissing] you. But Allah is not shy of the truth. *And when you ask [his wives] for something, ask them from behind a partition.* That is purer for your hearts and their hearts. And it is not [conceivable or lawful] for you to harm the Messenger of Allah or to marry his wives after him, ever. Indeed, that would be in the sight of Allah an enormity.

Indeed, in this case, the second version actually seems to make more sense!

Seventh, the idea that Almighty God strikes deals with human beings, whereby he gives them paradise in exchange for their money and possessions, which they invest in jihad in the cause of Allah strikes me as odd. Why would God seek to enrich himself financially by gifts from mere sinful mortals? The nature of Muslim paradise is another problem in itself, to be mentioned in the subsequent point, which does not sit comfortably with the idea of a righteous holy God.

Today, I understand that God does not need anything from us, nor does he allow anyone to purchase a ticket to paradise. As the Bible says, "May your money perish with you, because you thought you could buy the gift of God with money!" (Acts 8:20), and "For the wages of sin is death, but the gift of God is eternal life in Christ Jesus our Lord" (Romans 6:23).

As I mentioned in my story, and in sharp disagreement with the Bible, the "deal" outlined inside the Quran is this:

Indeed, Allah has purchased from the believers their lives and properties [in exchange] for that they will have Paradise. They fight in the cause of Allah, so they kill and are killed. [It is] a true promise [binding] upon Him in the Torah and the Gospel and the Quran. And who is truer to his covenant than Allah? So, rejoice in your transaction, which you have contracted. And it is that which is the great attainment.[52]

As Sheikh 'Abū-l A'lā Maududi says in commenting on this verse,

The terms of this transaction from Allah's side are these: "If you voluntarily (and not by compulsion or coercion) agree to acknowledge that your life, your property and everything in this world, which in fact belong to Me, are Mine, and consider yourself only as their trustee, and voluntarily surrender the freedom I have given you to behave, if you so like, in a dishonest way and yourself become their master and owner, I will give you, in return, Gardens in the eternal life of the Next World." The one who makes this bargain with Allah is a Believer, for Faith is in fact the other name for making this bargain. On the other hand, the one who refuses to make this bargain, or after making it adopts the attitude of the one who has not made the bargain, is a *kafir*, for, technically, *kufr* is the term applied to the refusal to make this bargain.[53]

Commenting on this verse, Ibn Kathīr wrote,

> Allah states that He has compensated His believing servants for
> their lives and wealth—if they give them up in His cause—with
> Paradise. This demonstrates Allah's favor, generosity and bounty,
> for He has accepted the good that He already owns and bestowed,
> as a price from His faithful servants. Al-Hasan Al-Basrī and
> Qatadah commented, "By Allah! Allah has purchased them and
> raised their worth." Shimr bin ʿAtiyyah said, "There is not a Muslim
> but has on his neck a sale that he must conduct with Allah; he
> either fulfills its terms or dies without doing that." He then recited
> this Ayah. This is why those who fight in the cause of Allah are said
> to have conducted the sale with Allah, meaning, accepted and
> fulfilled his covenant (Allah's statement).[54]

So, it is a price for my soul, that I do not believe is a fair deal.

Eighth, it is a very strange thing to claim that the same God who
forbids things like alcohol and multiple sexual partners on earth not
only *permits* these exact things in paradise, but actually *provides*
them to those who have entered there.

Today, I understand that the true God would not say that wine is
utterly forbidden and from Satan. The Bible says of Jesus, "Once
more he visited Cana in Galilee, where he had turned the water into
wine..." (John 4:46). In sharp disagreement with the Bible, at least
concerning wine, the Quran says, "O you who believe! Wine,
gambling, altars and divining arrows are filth, made up by Satan.
Therefore, refrain from it, so that you may be successful."[55]

So, in one place—as above—the Quran says that wine is from
Satan, and elsewhere the same Quran says it is from Allah, as
implied in another Quran verse, "Indeed, for the righteous is attainment, Gardens and grapevines, And full-breasted [companions] of
equal age, And a full cup." Not only wine, but also women in their
youth, and with tempting bodies! I do not believe, however, that
heaven will have temptation and sexual relations.

Ninth, I found it hard to believe that works and good deeds
could save me because, if that were so, people would be judged

according to their capabilities and circumstances, which they are not responsible for in the first place. If God were truly just, then how could he hold people accountable for their actions, when people may have different abilities and not be equally able to do the things that the Quran and Hadith state are required to earn God's favor? People with mental or physical disabilities in Islam are constantly wondering how they are ever going to manage to avoid Hell. The Islamic system has tried to address this matter by stating that in such instances, one's *intentions* are what matter, but to me, this is an exception which simply proves the enormous theological problem of the system of justification by works.

Today, I have come to understand that salvation is by grace, through faith in Jesus Christ, not by works, so that no one should boast (Ephesians 2:8-9). According to the Bible, no one is able to be justified by his or her own actions and merits in God's sight. This is the entire reason for the biblical system of sacrifice in the first place. As the Bible states, "all have sinned and fall short of the glory of God," (Romans 3:23) and "the wages of sin is death" (Romans 6:23). "Without shedding of blood, there is no forgiveness" (Hebrews 9:22).

An animal sacrifice is ultimately insufficient to cover human sin —the system of the Passover and all subsequent animal sacrifices served a symbolic function, all ritually pointing forward to the one sufficient sacrifice of a pure and spotless Lamb (Jesus), matching our image (since we were made in His), and sinless so that His innocent blood could cover the sin of others. As Abraham told Isaac when the young boy asked, "'Father ... behold, the fire and the wood, but where is the lamb for the burnt offering?' Abraham said, 'God will provide for Himself the lamb for the burnt offering, my son.'" (Genesis 22:7-8).

Thanks be to God, that His love is not conditioned upon our ability. God's love, like his law, is pure and perfect. If God were to love only those who did good, then what human would ever be loved by Him? As everyone knows, the sort of love that is merely transactional is the weakest possible form of love. It is not selfless and caring; it is petty and selfish. God is not like that. His love is generous and abundant, and that is why David, a sinful man who had even committed adultery and then killed the husband of Bathsheba to hide his offense, was yet able to say, "You prepare a table before me in the presence of my enemies; My cup overflows" (Psalm 23:5). What wonderful news for you and I, who stand so equally in need of God's perfect love and forgiveness!

So, as demonstrated already, the Quran asserts that God loves only people who do good. But there are people who are different in their passion, energy, powers, and intelligence. For sure, there are people who are capable of doing more than others. So, if I am not as capable as others, then I will not be able to get what they will get in heaven or attain the degree that they will achieve.

Tenth, I couldn't see the logic of both Christianity and Islam being true. The two are polar opposites in their essential tenets. Therefore, if one is right, the other must be wrong.

Today, I understand that my sense was completely correct. These two religions *cannot* both be true. One of them (the Christian faith) is right, and the other (Islam) is wrong.

Eleventh, from 30 to 36 AD, a number of highly unlikely events occurred over a very short six years' time, that demonstrate the Christian message is true.

1. The Gospel was preached directly and very soon after Jesus' resurrection. **(Homologia)**
2. James, Jesus' brother came to be a believer in his message.
3. The pre-Pauline **creed. (1 Cor 15: 1-8)**
4. Saul, the fierce persecutor of the Christians, came to the Lord (becoming Paul) and made his first trip to Jerusalem, where he met the apostles and was confirmed in his teachings.

Today, I understand that the evidence supporting the Christian message is overwhelming. If Jesus Christ has been crucified, as I proved before, and resurrected, then Christianity is true, and if Christianity is true, then Islam cannot ever be correct.

The resurrection, in particular, is a focal point in Christianity. It is also the central theological point. Paul emphasized this when he wrote, "And if Christ has not been raised, then our preaching is in vain and your faith is in vain." (I Corinthians 15:17)

Resurrection is proven by the biblical narrative. Namely, the following elements give strong support to the veracity of the message:

1. Jesus died by crucifixion
2. The disciples believed
3. The disciples' lives were transformed
4. The resurrection was preached very early
5. James' (the brother of Christ) and Paul's transformation

So, we can demonstrate the crucifixion and resurrection from the Bible, but the question is, can we prove the resurrection of Jesus from outside the Bible?

The answer is yes! A full and robust presentation of the evidences for the resurrection of Jesus has recently been published by Gary Habermas, and readers are highly encouraged to become familiar with it.[56] This small book is no place to lay out all the details that Habermas has catalogued, but rather to summarize these evidences.

A first evidence is that Christ rose and left the tomb empty. The most important evidence is the empty tomb that remains to this day, free of the bones of the dead, and which testifies to the resurrection of Christ. There are many evidences that have now been discovered and catalogued which reveal inscriptions and decorations, whether painted on the remains of the ruins of ancient churches, or archaeological icons that tell the story of the resurrection, but I find that the archaeological evidence that stands firm is that empty tomb in Jerusalem, which is now near a bus station a few hundred yards outside the Damascus Gate.

Michael Grant concludes, "The historian...cannot justifiably deny the empty tomb," since the normal exercise of historical research argues that "the evidence is firm and plausible enough to necessitate the conclusion that the tomb was indeed found empty."[57]

A second evidence for the resurrection is the shroud, popularly known to the world today as the Shroud of Turin (because of where it is now kept), the details of which all but confirm that it is the shroud of Christ and that the one who was buried in it rose after his burial. Two scholars, Keynes Stevenson and Gary Habermas, have given the shroud close attention. They designed an analytical methodology and concluded that if we apply the probability theory to the shroud, even using conservative estimates, the likelihood that it wrapped the body of a person other than Jesus Christ of Nazareth is equal to the result of multiplying the probabilities of the various factors present in the shroud that point to recorded facts about Jesus' crucifixion and resurrection (e.g., the pierced side, the crown of thorns, the lack of broken bones, and many other factors). They note that the likelihood of all the necessary factors in the same artefact if the shroud wrapped someone *other than* Jesus of Nazareth is approximately one in 83 million. Of course, this means that, while it remains theoretically possible that this shroud wrapped a person other than Christ, the likelihood—as a practical matter—approaches zero. They concluded, "There is no practical probability that someone other than Jesus Christ was buried in the Shroud of Turin."[58]

The third evidence for the resurrection is ancient pictures and inscriptions. There are numerous traces of oil paintings and inscriptions on pieces of wood and stone, dating back to the first and second centuries, indicating that Christ rose from the dead, and ascended alive to heaven with his body. Many scholars have published photographs of these images and inscriptions, such as Sir William Ramzy, in his book *Modern Discoveries and the Authenticity of the New Testament.*

The fourth evidence for the resurrection is archaeological copies of the Bible. There are many copies of the Bible dating back to the first centuries. Papyri fragments survive that scholars generally agree date to near the turn of the first century AD, such as P46, P52 and others. We also have manuscripts such as Washington, and papyri, which are many, and even translations dating back to the second century, such as the Assyrian, which dates back to the year 168 AD, and ancient Latin translations from the middle of the second century AD, as well as numerous papyri and manuscripts dating back to the third century AD, as well as translations such as Coptic Upper Egypt (Saidi), Buhairi, and others.

Among the manuscript evidence for both the Old and New Testaments are a collection of manuscripts and fragments discovered in caves at Qumran, near the Dead Sea. Many of them were produced before the time of Christ. One very helpful thing about those manuscripts from this group that were produced before the first century is that they demonstrate that, for example, the book of Isaiah was not altered in order to make its strong messianic prophecies more clearly descriptive of Jesus. No, the prophecies were written before Christ, and we have solid manuscript evidence demonstrating so.

A fifth evidence for the resurrection is the testimony of some Jewish scholars and others about the resurrection of Christ, a topic that we turn to below.

Historians

Cornelius Tacitus

Living from 56 to the 117 AD, Tacitus was one of the greatest historians of the Roman state. A Roman himself, he was known for accuracy and integrity. He lived through the reigns of six emperors. One of his most famous books was the *Annals and Histories*. Many references to Christ and Christianity appear in his books, one of the most prominent being,

> "Consequently, to get rid of the report, Nero fastened the guilt and inflicted the most exquisite tortures on a class hated for their abominations, called Christians by the populace. Christus, from whom the name had its origin, suffered the extreme penalty during the reign of Tiberius at the hands of one of our procurators, Pontius Pilatus, and a most mischievous superstition, thus checked for the moment, again broke out not only in Judaea, the first source of the

evil, but even in Rome, where all things hideous and shameful from every part of the world find their center and become popular. Accordingly, an arrest was first made of all who pleaded guilty; then, upon their information, an immense multitude was convicted, not so much of the crime of firing the city, as of hatred against mankind. Mockery of every sort was added to their deaths. Covered with the skins of beasts, they were torn by dogs and perished, or were nailed to crosses, or were doomed to the flames and burnt, to serve as a nightly illumination, when daylight had expired. Nero offered his gardens for the spectacle, and was exhibiting a show in the circus, while he mingled with the people in the dress of a charioteer or stood aloft on a car. Hence, even for criminals who deserved extreme and exemplary punishment, there arose a feeling of compassion; for it was not, as it seemed, for the public good, but to glut one man's cruelty, that they were being destroyed."[59]

It is clear from this document that Christianity derived its name from Christ, and that Pontius Pilate was the one who sentenced him to death. The myth or rumor he alluded to is the resurrection.

Lucian the Greek Samosati

Lucian was one of the most prominent historians of Greece at the turn of the second century AD. He commented in a satirical critical article on Christians and Christ in the book "The Death of Bergernaut" by Lucian (born in 100 AD). This is a significant passage from his writings:

"The Christians, you know, worship a man to this day—the distinguished personage who introduced their novel rites, and was crucified on that account. ... You see, these misguided creatures start with the general conviction that they are immortal for all time, which explains the contempt of death and voluntary self-devotion which are so common among them; and then it was impressed on them by their original lawgiver that they are all brothers, from the moment that they are converted, and deny the gods of Greece, and worship the crucified sage, and live after his laws. All this they take quite on faith, with the result that they despise all worldly goods alike, regarding them merely as common property."[60]

Lucian also reported that the Christians had "sacred writings" which were frequently read. When something affected them, "they spare no trouble, no expense."[61]

Flavius Josephus

Living from 37 to 97 or 100 AD, Josephus was an acclaimed Jewish historian. Included in his book "The Dates," written 90-95 AD, is a paragraph on the crucifixion of Christ. In 1972, an Arabic manuscript was published, which scholars believe is an accurate translation of the original text. It states:

> At this time there was a wise man who was called Jesus. And his conduct was good and he was known to be virtuous. And many people from among the Jews and other nations became his disciples. Pilate condemned him to be crucified and to die. And those who had become his disciples did not abandon his discipleship. They reported that he had appeared to them three days after his crucifixion and that he was alive; accordingly, he was perhaps the messiah concerning whom the prophets have recounted wonders[62]

This testimony of Josephus preceded the testimony of the majority of pagan historians. And if we take into account that Josephus was famous among his peers for objectivity and that he dealt with this historical incident through Jewish data, it becomes clear to us that this text is a reportable text worthy of trust.

Gnostic sources

Gnosticism is a religious and philosophical movement dating back to the time before Christ. Its name comes from the Greek word *gnosis*, meaning knowledge. Gnosticism brings together various sects under its umbrella that differ in some principles and agree on others. This movement made knowledge—and in particular *secret* knowledge—the focal point of its religious beliefs. During the second century AD, when Christianity was spreading, Gnostics began to take a lot of what suited their thinking, and overlay their worldview onto the Christian scriptures. One core belief of the Gnostics was that the body is evil, and is only a prison for the soul. The Gnostics therefore asserted that Christ did not take an evil body, but it was somehow a gelatinous body, and also the idea that the crucified body was only a likeness of the Messiah. It seems to some that the Islamic view of Jesus was affected in part by the Gnostics in its concept of the crucifixion of Christ. However, similar teaching in Gnosticism was aiming at a purpose different from that of the Islamic religion. Gnosticism, or at least some of its sects, believed that Christ, a God incarnate, could not be crucified because his body differed from the bodies of humans. Therefore, the body that was actually crucified could not have been that of Christ. This is interesting, because Islam likewise does not deny the process of the Cross, but it merely denies that the crucified person was Christ. Islam makes this assertion not on the basis of the nature of Jesus' body, but rather on the basis that it was not proper for Christ to be crucified. Islamic tradition asserts, rather, that Jesus was raised to heaven by God's power before his enemies could arrest him, and God placed his likeness on another, who replaced him.

However, the study of the religious and literary effects of the Gnostic movement provides us with other evidence for the authenticity of the gospel narrative about the crucifixion and resurrection of Christ, especially what was mentioned in the early Gnostic literature, such as:

The Gospel of Truth, probably by Valentius, around 135-160 AD

"For when they had seen him and had heard him, he granted them to taste him and to smell him and to touch the beloved Son. When he had appeared instructing them about the Father. ... For he came by means of fleshly appearance." Other passages affirm that the Son of God came in the flesh and "the Word came into the midst ... it became a body."[63]

"Jesus, was patient in accepting sufferings ... since he knows that his death is life for many ... he was nailed to a tree; he published the edict of the Father on the cross. ... He draws himself down to death through life. ... eternal clothes him. Having stripped himself of the perishable rags, he put on imperishability, which no one can possibly take away from him."[64]

The Aprocryphon of John, probably by Saturninus, around 120-130 AD

"It happened one day when John, the brother of James, who are the sons of Zebedee—went up and came to the temple, that a Pharisee named Arimanius approached him and said to him, 'Where is your master whom you followed?' And he said to him, 'He has gone to the place from which he came.' The Pharisee said to him, 'This Nazarene deceived you with deception and filled your ears with lies and closed your hearts and turned you from the traditions of your fathers.'"[65]

The Gospel of Thomas, probably from 140-200 AD

Contains many references to, and alleged quotations of, Jesus.[66]

The Treatise On Resurrection, uncertain author, late second century, to Rheginos

"The Lord ... existed in flesh and ... revealed himself as Son of God ... Now the Son of God, Rheginos, was Son of Man. He embraced them both, possessing the humanity and the divinity, so that on the one hand he might vanquish death through his being Son of God, and that on the other through the Son of Man the restoration to the Pleroma might occur; because he was originally from above, a seed of the Truth, before this structure of the cosmos had come into being."

"For we have known the Son of Man, and we have believed that he rose from among the dead. This is he of whom we say, 'He became the destruction of death, as he is a great one in whom they believe.' Great are those who believe."

"The Savior swallowed up death. ... He transformed himself into an imperishable Aeon and raised himself up, having swallowed the visible by the invisible, and he gave us the way of our immortality."

"Do not think the resurrection is an illusion. It is no illusion, but it is truth. Indeed, it is more fitting to say that the world is an illusion, rather than the resurrection which has come into being through our Lord the Savior, Jesus Christ."

"... [A]lready you have the resurrection ... why not consider yourself as risen and already brought to this?" Rheginos was thus encouraged not to "continue as if you are to die."[67]

Although we have no reason to believe that God inspired these gospels—which are are late and in some cases contain material that would be heretical when measured by the standard of the canonical gospels, their authors often used the term 'gospel' in the plain meaning of that word (i.e., "good news") without implying that they were actual eyewitness accounts like those of the earlier gospel writers, they all mention that Christ is both God and man, and they serve as confirmation of the early perception of the truthfulness of Christ's crucifixion.

I end my words here with what has been said by the Jewish and Hebrew professor, Joseph Klausner who said in his book *Jesus of Nazareth*:

> "It is impossible to assume that there is a deception in the matter of the resurrection of Christ, because it is inconceivable that it remains a nineteen-century deception" (Klausner lived in the nineteenth century).[68]

After all these 'fast forwards,' I will continue relating my personal story. My heart started to lean toward Christianity, and I decided to take a crazy step, that is to get in touch with this pastor from whom I was learning. It was a major step for me. I decided to speak to him, and this conversation was one of the most bizarre I have ever had.

---

1. Al-Qurtubi, Muhammad ibn Ahmad. "Interpretation of Surat an-Nisā'." In *Tafsir al-Qurtubi*, edited by Abd Allah ibn Abd al-Muhsin al-Turki, 4:112-113, (Beirut: Dar Ihya al-Turath al-Arabi, n.d.)

2. Cornelius Tacitus, "Annals," in *The Annals and the Histories*, trans. Alfred John Church and William Jackson Brodribb (New York: Random House, 2003), 15.44.

3. Pliny the Younger, "Letters," in *Pliny: Letters and Panegyricus*, trans. Betty Radice (Cambridge, MA: Harvard University Press, 1969), 10.96-97.

4. Suetonius, "Lives of the Caesars," in *The Twelve Caesars*, trans. Robert Graves (New York: Penguin Classics, 2007), 48.

5. Julius Africanus, "Extant Fragments of the Five Books of the Chronography of Julius Africanus," in *Ante-Nicene Fathers*, vol. 6, eds. Alexander Roberts and James Donaldson (Peabody, MA: Hendrickson Publishers, 1994), 130.

6. Philopon, De., opif. mund. II 21, in Felix Jacoby. *Die Fragmente der Griechischen Historiker*. Martinus Nijhoff. 2004. Sect 257 f16, c, p. 1165.

7. Pseudo-Dionysius, "The Divine Names," in *Pseudo-Dionysius: The Complete Works*, trans. Colm Luibheid (New York: Paulist Press, 1987), 45-46.

8. Lucian of Samosata, "The Death of Peregrine," in *The Works of Lucian of Samosata*, trans. H. W. Fowler and F. G. Fowler (Oxford: Clarendon Press, 1905), p.243-248.

9. Phlegon. "Chronicles of the Days." Quoted in *George Syncellus, Theophanes, and Eusebius of Caesarea. Chronography*. Edited by Joseph Scaliger, p.188. Leiden: Ex Officina Plantiniana, Franciscum Raphelengium, 1606.

10. Phlegon. "Chronicles of the Days." Quoted in William Paley, "The Evidences of Christianity: In Three Parts." London: Printed for J. Faulder, 1796.

11. Celsus. "The True Research." In The Ante-Nicene Fathers: Translations of the Writings of the Fathers down to A.D. 325, edited by Alexander Roberts and James Donaldson, vol. 4, 45. Edinburgh: T&T Clark, 1885

12. Josephus, Flavius. *Antiquities of the Jews*, Book 18, Chapter 3, Paragraph 3. Translated by William Whiston. Project Gutenberg, 2008.

13. Ibid., Book 20, Chapter 9, Section 1., p. 449.

14. Mara bar Serapion, Letter to His Son, trans. Robert McQueen Grant, in The Anchor Bible Dictionary, ed. David Noel Freedman (New York: Doubleday, 1992), vol. 4, p. 1029.

15. H. Polano (Tr.). *The Talmud: Selections from the Contents of That Ancient Book, Its Commentaries, Teachings, Poetry, and Legends*. Amsterdam: Philo Press, 1943, p. 42.

16. *Toledot Yeshu*, Manuscript, British Library, London.

17. Bruce M. Metzger. *The Text of the New Testament: Its Transmission, Corruption, and Restoration*. (New York: Oxford University Press, 2005), pp. 45-47, 287-288.

18. Surat al-Isrā' (Quran chapter 17), verse 59

19. Surat al-Anʿām (Quran chapter 6), verse 37

20. Surat ar-Raʾd (Quran chapter 13), verse 7

21. Surat Yūnus (Quran chapter 10), verse 20

22. Surat al-ʿAnkabūt (Quran chapter 29), verse 51

23. https://lunarscience.nasa.gov/?question=evidence-moon-having-been-split-two

24. Alfred Guillaume. *The Life of Muhammad: A Translation of Ibn Isḥāq's Sīrat Rasul Allah*. (Oxford: Oxford University Press, 2004), 659-660.

25. Surat Ali ʿImrān (Quran chapter 3), verse 28

26. As used in this verse, the word *allies* means people who are associated or connected by a close personal relationship such as friendship, love, or being socially close.

27. Al Māʾida (Quran chapter 5), verse 51

28. *Tafsīr Ibn Kathīr*

29. *Saḥīḥ al-Bukhārī*, Vol. I, Book 2, Hadith 25

30. *Saḥīḥ Muslim*, Book 26, Number 5389

31. *shirk*: Ascribing partners to God. In the Muslim way of thinking, the central biblical doctrine of the Trinity is *shirk*, as does (by extension) the Bible itself because it is the source of that doctrine. Therefore, the Christians who agreed to this document promised to keep this aspect their faith to themselves, never mention it in public, and never invite anyone to read or believe the Bible to be true.

32. An agreement that gives Christians, Jews, and Zoroastrians immunity from being killed by Muslims for the crime of existing, so long as they agree to live with abridged rights as tributaries (paying the *jizya* annually), and to abide by the constricting demands that the Muslims place upon them. The *dhimma* is sometimes called a "pact of protection," because it protects the subjected *dhimmis* from outside threats as well as from Muslims.

33. Jacob Marcus. *The Jew in the Medieval World: A Sourcebook, 315-1791*. New York: JPS (1938), 13-15.

34. Surat al-Ḥijr (Quran chapter 15), verse 9

35. Surat an-Naḥl (Quran chapter 16), verse 43

36. Surat al-Anbiyāʾ (Quran chapter 21), verse 105

37. Surat Ali ʿImrān (Quran chapter 3), verse 3

38. Surat Fuṣṣilat (Quran chapter 41), verse 43,

39. *Saḥīḥ al-Bukhārī*, Book of Virtues, 510

40. *Saḥīḥ al-Bukhārī*, Chapter 3, "Jamʾi al-Qurʾān," hadith no. 4986 (see also Ibn Abī Dawūd, *Kitāb al-Maṣāḥif*, p. 6-9)

41. *Saḥīḥ al-Bukhārī*, 6:60:201:

42. *Saḥīḥ al-Bukhārī*, Vol. 6, p. 478

43. The Brief Islamic Encyclopedia. "V26, P8175"

44. *Fatḥ al-Bārī* 8/743

45. *The Brief Islamic Encyclopedia* "V26, P8179"

46. Shia is one of the major sects of Islam that predominates in Iran, Yemen, Bahrain, and some other places. Its structure of authority and succession from Muhammad, as well as many of its secondary written material, is different from that of Sunni Islam.

47. Daniel Brubaker, *Corrections in Early Qurʾān Manuscripts: Twenty Examples*. Lovettsville: Think and Tell. 2019; Daniel Brubaker, "Forgotten God? —Post-production Insertions of Allāh in Early Qurʾān Manuscripts," in *Die Entstehung einer Weltreligion VI*. Berlin: Hans Schiler & Tim Mücke GbR. 2021; Daniel Brubaker, "A Critical Edition of the Qurʾān," in *Die Entstehung einer Weltreligion VII*. Berlin: Hans Schiler & Tim Mücke GbR. 2023; Daniel Brubaker, "Manu-

scripts and memory: the fraught nature of an obvious investigation into the textual history of the Quran," *Bibliotheca Orientalis* LXXVII, 5/6 (2020)

48. Muslims count their prayers in Islam by how many kneelings they must to do.
49. Surah Ali ʿImrān (Quran chapter 3), verses 31-32
50. See *The Brief Islamic Encyclopedia*, V26, P8188
51. The Hijra was the famous migration, from Mecca to Medina, of the early community of believers in Muhammad's message that, according to Islamic tradition, occurred in 622 AD. The Hijra came to mark the beginning of the Islamic calendar, which is designated by the abbreviation A.H. Thus, the year 622 AD became for the early community the year 1 AH.
52. Surah at-Tawba (Quran chapter 9), verse III
53. "Surah 9. At-Tauba. Aya III." https://www.alim.org/quran/tafsir/maududi/sura/9/111/#sdfootnote107anc
54. Ibn Kathīr. *Tafsīr Ibn Kathīr* (Abridged), Volume 10, Surat al-Ahzāb to the end of the Surahs, Abridged by a group of scholars under the supervision of Shaykh Safiur-Rahman al-Mubarakpuri, (Darussalam Publishers & Distributors, 2000), p. 381.
55. Surat al-Māʾida (Quran chapter 5), verse 90
56. Gary Habermas. *On the Resurrection: Evidences*. Brentwood: B&H Academic. 2024.
57. Michael Grant. *Jesus: An Historian's Review of the Gospels*. New York: Scribner. 176.
58. Stevenson, K. E. and G. R. Habermas. "Verdict on the Shroud: Evidence for the Death and Resurrection of Jesus Christ." Ann Arbor: Servant Books. (1981) 127-8.
59. Tacitus. *The Annals of Tacitus: Books 13-16*. Edited by R. H. Martin and A. J. Woodman, Cambridge University Press, 1986.
60. Lucian of Samosata. "The Death of Peregrine." In *Lucian, with an English Translation* by A. M. Harmon, vol. 3, pp. 34-35. Cambridge, MA: Harvard University Press, 1961.
61. Ibid.
62. Josephus. *Antiquities of the Jews*. Book 18, Chapter 3, Paragraph 3. William Whiston (Tr.). www.gutenberg.org/files/2828/2848-h/2848-h.htm#link18noteref-8
63. *The Gospel of Truth*. Translated by Robert M. Grant in The Nag Hammadi Library in English, edited by James M. Robinson, 3rd edition, HarperOne, 1990, pp. 23-25.
64. Ibid.
65. The Aprocryphon of John, in *The Nag Hammadi Library in English*, ed. James M. Robinson (San Francisco: Harper & Row, 1988), 140.
66. *The Gospel of Thomas*. Edited and translated by Marvin W. Meyer, (San Francisco: Harper, 1992).
67. "The Nag Hammadi Library: The Treatise on the Resurrection." Malcolm L. Peel (Tr.). http://gnosis.org/naghamm/res.html
68. Klausner, Joseph. *Jesus of Nazareth: His Life, Times, and Teaching*. Translated by Herbert Danby. (Bloch Publishing Company, 1946), p. 369.

7

WHAT IF?

I dreamed I was a butterfly, flitting around in the sky; then I awoke. Now I wonder: Am I a man who dreamt of being a butterfly, or am I a butterfly dreaming that I am a man?

— ZHUANGZI

In the end, I decided that learning the truth would be worth risking the hypothetical outcomes that were churning around in my head: What if he informed the police about me? What if he thought that I was lying? What if he asked me to do something that put my life in danger? Aware that (as he had mentioned several times) he mostly did not answer private inquiries anyway, in a moment of courage I opened a chat box and sent the pastor a message.

To my surprise, he replied immediately with an odd query: "Have you seen Him?" I was astonished. "What are you talking about?" He answered, "That person you are going to ask me about."

I wondered, it true that Christians engage in *magic*, as the rumor circulates among Muslims?

I asked, "How did you know that I had seen someone?"

He answered with another question, "Would you like to meet me?"

Now I was scared. "Where?" I replied.

"In my church."

"Me? No! How? I can't," I exclaimed.

He asked, "Because of the way you look?"

Again, I asked myself, "How could he know what I looked like?" (I had a prayer sign on my forehead and an obvious Salafi beard at that time.)

I typed, "How did you know how I look?"

He laughed. "My church is old and open for everyone, do not worry. Come! I want to meet you. Let's make it Friday at the time of Muslim prayer."

Then he sent the address and his personal phone number, and went offline.

The decision whether to go or not would be complicated! But I was curious how this man knew all that about me. Also, I wanted even more the answer to a fundamental question about my dreams: Why me?

So, I went to meet this pastor. I was particularly frightened since his church was close to a mosque. As I approached, I felt that everyone was looking at me, that I was odd and obvious. This man, however, was welcoming and he set me at ease. After exchange of pleasantries, he asked me, "What happened, and who are you?"

So, I shared my story, complete with the various details that you've just read. He listened until I came to the part of the dreams, and then I asked him my burning question, "Why me?"

His reply came across as quite strange. He asked, "When you asked Jesus to come to you, did He come?"

I said, "Yes!"

He said, "Then, ask him again, why me? It seems like a personal relationship, so I should not interfere."

By the time I left the pastor, and although I did not feel that he had helped increase my knowledge, I felt that my love for Jesus had only increased—and my desire to know what he wanted from me grew in tandem. Could Christianity be the answer?

I started to visit this pastor every second week to talk about the Christian faith, and he gave me homework—something to do every time.

I learned to pray to Jesus for the first time in my life. Since all my life I had been immersed in the Islamic view of Jesus, that he is only a man and should not receive the sort of reverence due only to God, praying to him was not easy at first. But as I began reading the Bible, I began to believe its authenticity—and that Jesus is not only the son of God but actually God in the flesh—as he clearly claimed in his teaching and his answers to those inquiring of him.

At that time, I was still leading Muslim prayers at the mosque and attending my Islam lessons! However, I abandoned my secret, sinful nocturnal life. I was busy reading the Bible—on my computer—and getting some small books about Christianity, which I would read under the blanket after everybody in my house had gone to sleep. I was truly scared, but enjoyed every word I read. The love and the beauty of Christianity were so amazing to me.

Meanwhile, I was afraid to share my new thoughts with anyone except one person, a trusted friend with whom I could share anything without fear. I started to feel that I was changing into an ordinary Christian; I began to love people, I no longer harbored hatred for anyone, I wanted everyone to get saved—and most importantly, I felt that a personal relationship was forming between God (my Creator!) and myself.

Soon, I decided to get baptized, but the pastor was hesitant to baptize me yet, which made me angry. So, I made contact with another Christian from the same room in a chat room on an app called Paltalk, and asked him to help me. And he did help me...but it proved to be a mistake.

My baptism was such a stressful event. Everyone was afraid on that day. Was I a spy? Was it safe to take a person like me into the fold? The church was afraid of my family's reaction and also that of the security services. In order to ensure complete secrecy, they asked me to change trains twice on the way to the venue. Then they asked me to meet them in a crowded place, where they took me into a car with dark windows. I was taken to a church under construction to be baptized.

It felt like I was an agent in "Mission, Impossible!" However, it was indeed a bold and dangerous step.

Initially, this person was not ready at all to help me. He was very kind, but he was also spiritually immature. Unfortunately, he turned out to be the cause of many problems for me in the coming days. For example, he would call me at home to ask about me, and he forgot that my family knew all the groups that I belong to. It was strange for them to have someone with a strange name calling to ask about me.

Secondly, I had not been ready for baptism. I was still grappling with the "what if" question. Every time I prayed, I was still wondering, "What if I'm wrong? What if I've lost my way again? How can eternity be guaranteed? How can I be reassured that I'm really on the right path?" It was a strenuous period of uncertainty, which made it difficult for me to focus on God.

Yes! That is exactly what happened; after a while, I became exhausted by the demands of the new pastor and the man who had introduced me to him; The constant prayers, learning, and many other impositions made me question whether I had actually *left* Islam, since everything seemed to be ritualistic and there was far too heavy an emphasis being placed on works by my new-found Christian friends.

This circumstance led me to begin to wonder whether the truth might lie in more ancient eastern religions, since I was no longer convinced it was to be found in Islam, Christianity or Judaism.

While browsing through a secular library one day, I found a book called "Tao Te Ching" by Lao Tzu. Looking through it, I encountered yet another perspective that was new for me...and I liked the ideas presented in the book and started to learn about Taoism. Among other things, I began to practice meditation. At the time, the movie "Eat, Pray and Love," was popular. I became convinced and I needed to get deeper into Taoism. I was hoping that the more meditation I did, the more peace and self-discovery I would achieve. But where could I find meditation classes?

I searched on the Internet for a meditation group and suddenly found a group of Indians doing meditation classes at their home, free of charge, once a week.

Having attended one of these classes in person, I was surprised by how great group meditation was. After one meeting, I tried to talk to the other group members in person, and found them to be very welcoming. I asked many questions about how we can find ourselves, how we can discover the truth, and how can we know that what we know is true? Their answers were profound, or at least they seemed deep to me at that time.

I loved attending these meditation classes, and the leaders started to give me books by someone called Newton, who was a guru —not the celebrated Newton the physicist. This Newton wrote about the science of meditation. I was also given books by Osho, who is one of the most important gurus in the last century and by someone important to them named "Bharamesh Patri ji." I read and learned a lot, and then asked more questions at the subsequent meeting. These people invited me to stay after meditation classes and to share their Indian food, and we became friends. I learned rapidly about many things including the "New Age." I did not mention anything about Jesus at that time. I was really confused! But, I wanted to conceal my confusion.

In my observation, New Age piques one's curiosity more than any other worldview, because it deals with secrets of the soul, knowing oneself, and reaching Nirvana—or whatever higher spirit one can be. I grew more curious about myself and continued to crave to know the truth about myself.

In order to do better group meditation and lead the group with music, I learned how to play the flute. These people soon let me lead the group, due to my fluency in Arabic, and my trust in them increased.

All was fine until something truly evil happened to me. I read an article about a guru called Vemena. Subsequently, I did my medita-tion during which I saw a spirit. Until that time, I had no idea that our practices could open the door to evil demonic spirits. This spirit that appeared spoke to me. He told me that he was "Vemena" and he was me, and that he wanted to be in me and me in him. This was so strange that I sought the advice of my friends. They advised me to come and talk to them urgently.

When I met with them, they asked me to tell the details of what I had experienced. And, as I shared, I noticed that they simply smiled.

Someone said to me, "You are the reincarnation of Vemena!" Now, I had read about reincarnation, but I never thought that I might become one. This incident was so significant for these New Agers, since they took it to mean that the reincarnated individual possesses all the wisdom and power of Vemena. Their attitude towards me became noticeably more respectful and reverent.

Some days after this incident, they told me that the great master Patri ji was coming to Egypt and wanted to meet me in person.

This news made me very happy, and I looked forward to the meeting. The meeting began with Patri ji his telling me, "You are an intelligent guy who can benefit us. I want you to consider yourself at home. We are your family, and we can do great things together."

Although I was uncomfortable with his talk, I was still curious to know what he actually meant by this statement.

He asked the Indian family if I should come to India to attend the great event, and that he would talk to me again there.

This was in the summer. At Christmastime, I told my family that I had a work trip to India, and I traveled to one of the most popular and significant events for meditators in the whole world called "Dyana Maha Chakram," the cosmic event of meditation. I was really excited to see this whole new world—80,000 people coming from across the globe to visit Hyderabad in order to do meditation.

On the third day after my arrival, Patri ji, asked me to share my story with New Age. When I did so, I noticed that people became really excited. On that day, they anointed me as a guru, and Patri ji announced me as the new Vemena and his reincarnation.

And it led to even more veneration! On the day of celebrating Vemena as a guru, Patri ji asked me to sit in front of the people, who then came to obtain my blessing. People started to see me in dreams, and I got the power of healing some people—which I now understand was demonic. I stayed with those people for one year, and when people began to bow at my feet, I was shocked and I started to be scared. After that, the gurus began to take me to their private meetings, where I now began to see the truth about their movement. My self-indulgent pleasure in being glorified as God came to be replaced with disappointment. I discovered that most of these gurus' children were living in America, not in Tibet or doing meditation in a cave. I saw how these people were controlling others under the guise of meditation and how it was, in reality, largely just a business. Upon this revelation, I decided to rethink the New Age as a worldview.

For people unfamiliar with New Age, let me explain. New Age is an expression of a supposed "new age" of spirituality—a blend of Hindu, Buddhist, Taoism, and various other Eastern religions that embrace polytheism. The New Age movement was developed to create a transition space for outside people who have never before experienced or embraced Eastern religions.

The New Age rests upon intellectual relativism, meaning that there is no absolute right or wrong. Instead, New Agers insist that truth is relative, that every person has the right to claim that they have "the truth"—and herein lies the problem. No one can have an exclusive claim on the truth. This fact is due to their subordination to the same ideas of the eastern religions, which is "the unity of existence" and "Oneness" that "all is in God and God is in all," meaning God is in me and you and in the cat, the goat, the cockroach, the earth and the piece of candy that you eat and the dung. Please forgive me; I give extreme examples to carry their proposition that we are all parts of God to its conclusion.

Osho, one of the most renowned leaders of the New Age movement, says: "If you do not feel that every time you cut a piece of candy and eat it, you are missing a part of yourself, then you are not enlightened, because everyone is one, and God is in everyone."

In time, they began to be more open about their belief that "God is energy."[1] Since all material in the universe has energy, if energy equals God, then that would mean that God is in all matter. Osho also wrote, "In existence you cannot make clear-cut divisions, everything melts into each other. It is oneness expressing in millions of ways; as a man, as a rose, as a fish ... it is the same life. And this is the mystery of life—that it can become a rose, and it can become a fish, and it can become a man, and it can become a buddha."[2] I also heard him state this in a lecture.

New Age movements also assert a positive pluralistic worldview, meaning that there is not just one way to God or the truth, but 'all roads lead to Rome,' so to speak. To a New Ager, then, when someone asserts one particular way to God as 'the truth' it is evidence that the person is not enlightened. The great irony of their position, of course, is that the assertion that there are many ways to God is itself an exclusive truth claim—for example, it excludes the possibility that ony one road leads to God. But the positive pluralistic worldview is their belief. Enlightenment, to a New Ager, is the greatest destination for any human being. This worldview is not new, but it continues to spread widely in Europe, America, Australia, and even the Arab countries. Many Egyptians subscribe to it. I personally know many individuals and organizations who promote the New Age movement in Egypt.

New Agers do not encourage explicit preaching. For this reason, you will not encounter a direct preacher or evangelist calling you to convert the New Age Movement. Instead, they tend to wait for signs that a person may have already begun to think along those lines.[3]

We start with the first basis of this system, which I mentioned previously, being absolute relativism:

The most fundamental tenet of New Age thinking is "absolute relativism," which is incidentally also advocated by Eastern religions, seen in atheistic, agnostic, and non-religious thought, in many ideas from all over the world. Though it is not my intention to generalize, most of them call for "absolute relativism." Is everything really relative in the absolute? Everyone sees the truth from his or her own point of view, so everyone is correct about his or her own position—that is the relativist's line of reasoning.

Unfortunately, one of the phrases we commonly repeat in daily parlance is "everything is relative." But this statement is not correct, for it implies that the truth is relative, that right and wrong are relative. If true, it would mean that we cannot have confidence in any of our moral senses. For instance, one person may consider that the living God exists; yet another may hold a polar opposite view, claiming that God does not exist. But both cannot be true, and this obvious fact renders relativism nonsensical. The New Age worldview rests upon utterly fallacious reasoning.

To take just one example of the pluralist worldview in Western popular culture, an article entitled "The Truth is Dead," was published in the American magazine *Time*. Though the headline sounds shocking, it was also ironically self-defeating, because how did anyone know whether the headline was truthful or not? If it is true, then it is false!

Then when someone says to you, "there is no absolute truth, all truth is relative," all you have to do is go back and say, "can there be a sentence stating that there is no absolute truth, that in itself is an absolute truth?"

If it is an absolute truth, you are a liar that there is no whole truth. If it is relative, it remains illogical because it is a sentence that negates itself. This sentence contradicts itself. It is a type of logical fallacy called a self-contradicting statement.

That is why many human values and principles were lost. People began to take advantage of this destructive idea which bears no relation to the real world. The natural consequence of the New Age Worldview is that everyone becomes self-referential. This leads to selfishness and arrogance. People act as though they are divine. But relativism of human principles and values has caused people to withdraw and isolate themselves, because what one person considers to be wrong or unbearable to commit, it may be that another person may believe it to be an acquired right, and that the opposite position is just a viewpoint.

Absolute relativism makes all personal experiences clash with the affairs of another person, and further makes it impossible to judge who is right and who is wrong, which renders the New Age worldview self-contradictory. Further, no matter how advanced you are in the knowledge of New Ageism, such a worldview will always remain a view which does not represent real people to real people.

Worse still, you can ascribe neither success nor failure to any action or human enterprise, because the New Age Movement provides no standard or canon as a point of reference.

I left the New Age movement for many reasons, not limited to its untenable relativism:

1. I couldn't believe that people's testimonies can constitute evidence for New Age, as different individuals are bound to contradict one another, which amounts to a shot in the foot. Moreover, making individuals the ultimate point of reference is essentially subjective. I believe moral value should be objective.
2. I couldn't believe that God can be a mere form of energy, because this notion bypasses the question of God choosing to create the world, an act which-presupposes a will and a person.
3. I couldn't believe that irrational power can create rational beings.
4. I couldn't believe that there is reincarnation for the same number of souls on the earth, while we have a massively increasing population worldwide.
5. I found it impossible to accept that my soul was similar to the souls of animals. It seems evident that, even if animals have souls, the human soul is somehow different. We never see a group of monkeys fighting for women's rights or economic justice.

Even from my study of Hinduism and Buddhism while I was involved with New Age, I also found them untenable. I do not believe in Hinduism because:

1. I couldn't believe that God, by definition, can be more than one; so, about 330 million Gods make no sense?
2. I couldn't believe that God could be a compound of three with different natures (Brahma, Vishnu, Shiva).
3. I couldn't believe in the holy book Vedas, the oldest manuscripts for which come from the 11th century (i.e., the

Devimahatmya Sanskrit MS, Nepal),[4] up to which point in time, it only existed as an oral tradition.

4. I couldn't believe anyone reached the "Moksha" salvation by unity with Brahma.
5. If reincarnation between the human and animal kingdom is true, how could a person be a good animal to return to being human or vice versa? On what basis can we say that a human or animal is better than another one?

When it came to Buddhism, I rejected it because:

1. I couldn't see the Gautama Buddha ever asking me to follow him, or claiming divinity.
2. I saw that the Gautama Buddha left his pregnant wife to seek wisdom and abdicate his responsibility towards his family, only to later regret his wrong doing.
3. I couldn't see that "life is suffering," as I understood Buddhism to assert. Indeed, life contains suffering, but it was not at all evident to me that life is equal to suffering.
4. I couldn't believe that attachment is the main reason for suffering. What matters is to whom one is attached. One further snag for me was that detachment could also be suffering.
5. There is no proof of the existence of Nirvana, as we have never seen anyone there.
6. In Buddhism, I am God, so why should I have righteousness via the Eight Noble Paths? And, who will even define righteousness? What if I, being God as Buddhism asserts, simply chose to define righteous speech as insulting others?
7. If pain is an illusion, one can hardly make such a ludicrous claims while sitting on a sharp stick? If pain were just an illusion, why do the vast majority of humans experience pain? And how do we all get it?
8. If reincarnation is true, and I relive my life in order to improve it and pay for my sins, why does my life end once

I get enlightened? What is the sense in ending a life once it is perfected?

After this long journey with New Age, I remembered that Jesus was the only person I loved, He is unique. I decided there was no one like Him. In addition, Christianity, according to what I studied, is the only worldview that really fulfills the minimum standards for a sound worldview, as James Sire says:

> A worldview is a commitment, a fundamental orientation of the heart, that can be expressed as a story or in a set of presuppositions (assumptions which may be true, partially true, or entirely false) which we hold (consciously or subconsciously, consistently or inconsistently) about the basic constitution of reality, and that provides the foundation on which we live and move and have our being.[5]

A correct worldview should be:

1. Logically valid
2. Internally coherent
3. Applicable to daily life

That's precisely what Christianity is! It answers life's four main existential questions logically, coherently, and in an applicable way.

1. Where did we come from? (i.e., the question of origin)
2. Why do we live? (i.e., the question of meaning)
3. How should we live? (i.e., questions of morality)
4. Where are we going to? (i.e., the question of destiny)

However, I had a problem with the church. The church's words and deeds did not seem to be consistent with each other. I did not want to become a nominal Christian who goes to church seeking to get blessed. I knew in my heart that there was something more. Until

I found out what that might be, I decided that I would worship Jesus as best I could.

---

1. Osho. *In Search of the Miraculous: Kundalini Yoga*. Vol. 2, No. 2 India: Sterling Publishers Pvt. Ltd (1997)
2. Osho. *The Zen Manifesto: Freedom From Oneself*. Cologne: Rebel Publishing House. (1993) Ch 8, Q 2 131.
3. See also: Bhagwan Shree Rajneesh. *99 Names of Nothingness*. New York: Osho International Foundation (1982)
4. Devi Mahatmyam is a text extracted from Markandeya Purana, and constitutes the latter's chapters 81 through 93. [23] The Purana is dated ot the ~3rd century CE,[10] and the Devi Mahatmyam was added to the Markandeya Purana either in the 5th or 6th century. Cheever Mackenzie Brown. *The Devi Gita: The Song of the Goddess: A Translation, Annotation, and Commentary*. New York: State University of New York Press (1998) 77, note 28.
5. James W. Sire. *Naming the Elephant: Worldview as a Concept*. Westmont: IVP Academic (2014), 122.

8

THE GOD OF HER DREAMS

My sheep hear my voice, and I know them, and they follow me. I give them eternal life, and they will never perish, and no one will snatch them out of my hand. My Father, who has given them to me, is greater than all, and no one is able to snatch them out of the Father's hand.

— JOHN 10: 27-29

In 2011, I was working as a learning and development specialist in one of the largest holdings of contact service centers in Egypt. One of the trainees, named Nancy, caught my attention. This girl was different. The moment I saw this Muslim girl, I had a premonition she would convert to Christ and become my wife. I do not know why I thought so, but this is the strong feeling I had the moment I saw her. I wanted to talk to her, but it was not easy at that time to do so. I kept looking at her the whole training period.

Also, in this season of my life, I was busier with faith problems than any other problem. I left Nancy and the company, and I traveled to India as I mentioned before.

During my last week in India, while in Bangalore, I received a message from Nancy. She asked me about these strange photos I was uploading to Facebook. I told her they were photos from India because I am abroad now, but coming back to Egypt next week and would be happy to meet with her. To my surprise, she agreed! I was so thrilled. I returned from India looking forward to meeting with her.

I was due to deliver a lecture to some students at the university, so I thought that it would be a good idea to meet Nancy there. I invited her to the lecture, which she attended, following which I invited her to dinner. At that time, Nancy was getting a kind of promotion at our company—my old company—to be a trainer, and she wanted to ask me how to be a better trainer. But this was the apparent intention. Her hidden agenda was to learn more about Islam from someone who had a profound understanding of Islam and had a TV program on a Salafi Channel.[1] Her motive was that she had begun to develop doubts about Islam. As for me, I wanted to see whether I still had the same feelings for her that I had had when I saw her for the first time.

We did not speak about training at all. Instead, we mainly asked about each other, India, meditation, and these things that I posted recently in the light of being a Salafi Muslim. We met several times subsequently, under the pretext of discussing training. But, we never really spoke about training. Whenever I was with Nancy, I took care to appear normal. For example, when I was with a group of people and heard the call to prayer, I went to pray. Not so with Nancy. I was so neutral when we were talking about God or human beings. Then one day, Nancy asked me an unexpected question, "How can you be a Salafi but not answer the call to prayer?" My immediate answer was, "Who told you that I am not praying?"

She said, "You are with me now, and the prayer call was 15 minutes ago, and you did not go to pray."

I said, "Umm, what do you mean precisely by praying?"

She said, "Praying! Muslim praying. Standing and bowing. This stuff!"

"Ah! But do you think that this is praying?" I said. She asked me to explain.

I said, "I believe that prayer is much deeper than we think. It is much deeper than repeating some words that we have memorized. Prayer is a relationship we need to have with God, one which needs to grow in depth, until we meet God Himself."

Nancy's eyes shone with delight, as if she had been hoping for such an answer. As our conversation grew in profundity, she asked me, "How do you see God?"

My answer was, "I see him as beautiful, beyond our perception or comprehension. More loving and more patient, and generally amazing."

Every time we met after that, we spoke about the attributes of God. Nancy and I started to have feelings for each other. These feelings became undeniable and hard to hide. Nor did we try to conceal these feelings. It must have been these strong feelings which gave Nancy the courage to, one day, declare to me: "Look, I want to share a secret with you." I paused in anticipation.

She continued, "What I have to say may surprise or even provoke you to anger. Please do not show anger or disappointment towards me!"

I told her, "I cannot be angered by anything Nancy tells me."

She said, "I am not a Muslim. I will never be a Muslim, and I will not marry a Muslim guy or have Muslim kids."

I could feel a big smile dawn on my face and said, "Neither am I!"

Nancy was pleasantly surprised by my response. She was firmly convinced that I was Salafi Muslim. She must have wondered how I could *not* be a Salafi Muslim.

The thought now occurred to me: What would I do if Nancy also did not want to marry a Christian, or if she hated Christianity as most Muslims do?

For this reason, I decided not to tell her that I was a Christian yet. Instead, I said, "I am still searching, Nancy. I am not sure exactly where the truth is. Would you like to explore the subject with me?"

She said, "Sure, what are you searching for now?"

I said, "Look, Islam is wrong, as we know. Atheism needs more faith than theism and is far from true. The same is true for Agnosticism and Deism, and please do not waste your life searching in Eastern religions. So, now I am looking into Christianity as it has both Jewish and Christian holy text together in one book. Would you like to explore with me?"

She said, "Yes!"

I told her, "Ok, then let us start from the beginning. In the beginning, God created heaven and Earth." I started to work through the Bible with Nancy. We studied the major prophets and characters: Adam, his children, Noah, Abraham, David, and Jesus. After nine months of meetings, we began to discuss the early church. Nancy suddenly stopped me and said, "It is enough." I did not know what she meant. She said, "Can't you see it? I have found the God of my dreams. I want to be a Christian."

I was so happy then, but I did not want to show it. I said, "OK, are you sure?" She said she was very confident. I said, "OK, I am not an expert on Christianity, but I know someone who might be able to help." At that point, I decided to call my old pastor, with whom I had only had occasional contact. I told him what had happened and what I had done. He told me to bring Nancy to his church.

Nancy was so stressed that day and did not know what to do; she did not feel comfortable with the idea of being alone with a pastor who may ask her private questions.

I tried to reassure her, but I was not certain how reassured she felt. However, once we met the pastor, Nancy only took five minutes to ask to talk with him alone! Meantime, unbeknownst to her, I was at the church praying for her. After three hours, Nancy and the pastor asked me to join them again. I was surprised when the pastor asked Nancy if she wished to get baptized. He actually was encouraging her by saying, "Nancy, your words, your way, everything about you is very Christian. You know what we believe and why we believe it, so would you like to get baptized now?"

Nancy looked at me as if to ask me to help her formulate a response. But I held my peace and maintained a poker face. So, she asked me directly for an opinion.

I advised Nancy, that this was her relationship with God, not mine. She should make her own decision, as we had already agreed that no one should try to influence the other person's decision. Nancy made up her own mind. She consented to the pastor and asked to be baptized. Although I was delighted, I had to conceal my true feelings for now.

Nancy got baptized. Once the ceremony and the service were over, Nancy found me crying. When she asked me for the reason, I said, "I do not know! Maybe because, at last, you made it." The Pastor asked her and me to join him in the church hall. Then he came up with another surprise. He declared, "Nancy, now would you like to marry Thomas?"

She replied, "But he is not a Christian!"

He laughed and said, "Who told you that? He has been a Christian for a long time."

This daring revelation by the pastor caused me grave concern, as it may have made Nancy feel that I had deceived her all this time. Instead she gave me a huge hug and asked why I had not revealed this to her before. I told her that I wanted her to come to Christ for Christ's sake, not for mine. Then I proposed to her, and she agreed to marry me. I was thrilled that Nancy agreed to be my wife.

We got married that day in the church. That was the easy part. The difficult part was, how could we, as ex-Muslims, get marriage certificates? The legal intricacies of this question for those living in a Muslim country like ours, cannot be overstated.

We each went back to our own homes, but agreed that I should visit her and ask for her hand in marriage from her father. A few days later, I made the journey, met her father and asked for her hand in marriage. But her father turned me down citing my strict Salafi reputation as the reason for his rejection. He feared since he and his family were liberal, Nancy would not be happy with me. Notwithstanding, Nancy's mom agreed to the marriage.

The next obstacle was to tell my family, especially my mother. My mom's reaction was hilarious. She, who had come across Nancy entirely by chance once before, called Nancy a belly dancer because she wore trousers and no hijab.[2] I humored my mother and confirmed that it was the same girl. My mom was not very happy with my choice of a wife. She said, "Ok then, you may marry Nancy, on condition that you leave this house, and never return to it again. I do not know you."

Though I was extremely hurt by my mother's rejection of me, a still small voice inside me told me to leave whilst I had a chance. I went into my room, gathered all my stuff, left my apartment keys to everything, and I left fully knowing there was no going back.

My mom looked perplexed by the reality of my departure. I think she hoped it would be a temporary departure and that I would regret my decision and return home. Little did she know that I would be gone forever!

When she realized I was serious, she started to curse me with very hard words and awful curses. She would say, "May you die before you marry her, may you not have kids with her, and if she gives you children, may they be deformed or handicapped." These curses, especially coming from a loving mother, felt so harsh and crushing.

They are indelibly etched in my memory, although I know that I am protected by the blood of Christ and no amount of cursing will touch me. But for one's own mother to curse him, when her duty and pleasure is normally to bless and nourish him, is immeasurably hurtful.

I called Nancy, and we decided that we should marry legally soon. Staying alone in our future apartment was a good opportunity to reflect on all that had happened and to ponder over what God had in store for us. I felt led by the Spirit and that I was beginning to lose many things for following Christ, including my family. I would miss my mom, my two brothers and my aunts. However, I felt that it was time for me to be released in order to fulfill the mission to which God had called me. Though I was giving up so much, one thing is certain: I was gaining much more.

"For what does it profit a man to gain the whole world and forfeit his soul?" Mark 8:36

After a few days, I called Nancy's mother by phone. She had met me a couple of times before, and I told her: I will marry your daughter tomorrow. Are you coming?

She answered in the affirmative.

We were wedded legally in a Muslim ceremony, as we are not allowed to get married by the church in a legal way as we had planned, and we moved together into a new apartment. My Nancy and I knew that God was with us.

---

1. I used to do a program for youth to develop, evangelize and help them to understand the beauty of Islam.
2. My mom refers to Nancy as "the belly dancer" because Nancy wears pants, which is not the Islamic custom.

9

THE SMALL CAGE IS OPENED TOWARD FREEDOM

I have said all these things to keep you from falling away. They will put you out of the synagogues. Indeed, the hour is coming when whoever kills you will think he is offering service to God.

— JOHN 16: 1-2

Once we moved in to our own place after getting married, life seemed to improve! Being together afforded us the chance to read the Bible as a couple and to be welcoming as Christians, at least in this small space we called our apartment. We could invite non-Christian friends and evangelize them, as well as Christian friends with whom we could fellowship and pray. Our home became like a small church. Not that it was straightforward or without a snag. Among other things, we lived in the same building as Nancy's parents, who were still Muslim.

This season of our relationship was a time of growth, and genuine honest self-discovery. Nancy was so passionate about all the new rituals, which were alien to someone of her previous worldview; unlike me, she came from a nominal Muslim background. However, I appeared to her to be somewhat lazy, because I was not overly keen on rituals. She asked me why I was not too keen on attending church services. I explained that as much as I wanted to have fellowship with other Christians I wanted to move away from rituals, which had dominated my life as a Muslim. In response, Nancy suggested that we looked for a less ritualistic church.

I had my doubts about the existence of non-ritualistic churches, until one of Nancy's friends invited us to her church. It was there that I discovered my heart's desire as a Christian; I told the Lord that I no longer wanted to live my life my own way; *"I want to live my life according to your will, Lord Jesus."* That day, when I gave the rest of my life to Jesus Christ was special, and I was filled with emotions that I had never experienced before. I shed many tears, and I was aware they were tears of joy because I knew that I was just born again, from above! Being in that church made me realize that I was not insane for having doubts. I discovered that it was quite in order to ask any questions. I discovered that I was at liberty to ask questions and to get answers; this liberty was obvious from the preaching, the atmosphere, and everything about that congregation spoke freedom. I felt a warmth in my body, as if it were on fire. I was overcome by a powerful desire to live for God and for God alone!

Our pastor in this church, from whom I learned a lot, introduced me to a preacher there who is a great Christian apologist, and that man did a great favor for me; he introduced me to the writings and teaching of many great Christian apologists in the United States and England, including Dallas Willard, William Lane Craig, Mike Licona, Gary Habermas, Fred Sanders, C.S. Lewis, John Stott, J.P. Moreland, David Cook (my mentor during my M.A.), Jay Smith, Paul Copan, John Lennox, Os Guinness, Norman Geisler, and James Sire. Many of these men I am now honored to also know in person. They taught me so much, and their books and videos opened a new dimension I hadn't seen before. They taught me how to think, and how to go deeper into the Word of God.

Over time, we developed a reputation amongst the students, and people became suspicious of us. One day, while I was lecturing at one of the universities, I received a phone call from Nancy. She was very scared; she told me that she has just gotten a call from the secret police, who had threatened her and told her that she must persuade me to stop what I was doing.

She had asked the officer to explain what he meant and added that we were innocent. The officer told her that the police were aware of our evangelistic activities at university and in our apartment. The police officer added that it would not be his department that would put an end to our evangelistic activities, but rather my Salafi family, who would not hesitate to kill me if it were necessary. The police would continue to monitor our activities and keep my family abreast of our reaction to his threat.

Although I tried to reassure Nancy and encourage her not to worry too much, I myself was scared! It seemed impossible to continue to live in Egypt, under such circumstances. Egypt became like a huge jail, and we needed to escape by any means. It was necessary to go to another country where we could be Christians and be safe at the same time.

By God's grace, we managed to leave Egypt for a new country where we could practice our faith openly without fear of violence. After one week in the new country, I told Nancy that the time had come for us to be open about our faith in Christ. It was time we told everyone that Jesus is our only savior.

I wrote a post on Facebook saying that Nancy and I had become Christians and we believe that Jesus is our only Savior. Our world seemed to turn upside down; at that time, I had almost 5000 Facebook friends—99% of whom were Muslims. Most of them started attacking me verbally. They insulted her and threatened to kill me. In only one week, I received 359 direct death threats and numerous amounts of indirect ones. I even found out that my name had been published on Wikipedia as a well-known Muslim who had converted from Islam to Christianity.

Our escape to safety was a miracle. One week after we declared on Facebook that we were followers of Jesus, the Egyptian police arrested my mother-in-law and interrogated her demanding every detail from the moment I met Nancy's family until the day we left Egypt.

We thank God that she did not know anything about us, not even where we had escaped to. The police told both my mother-in-law, and my mother who had also been interrogated, that I stood accused of three crimes:

1. Defamation of religion.
2. Inciting sectarian strife.
3. Disturbing public security.

Despite all of this trouble, we decided that my Facebook account would continue as part of our ministry and for lifting the name of the Lord Jesus. We prayed that as a result, Muslims would enquire and learn about the Lord and get to know Him.

In the new country, it was not easy to establish ourselves as we started from the beginning. Part of me longed for my family, whom I love. After we got settled in and established, I called my mom.

When she took the phone, I said, "Hi, Mom! I pray that you are ok and everyone at home is fine."

She answered, "We are all fine, are you ok now?"

I said, "Yes! Very OK, by God's grace," and I continued, "How are my brothers Amr and Mostafa?[1] I so much want to talk to them. May I?"

"Never come close to your brothers!" she screamed at me, "Never try to call them! If you come close to them, I will kill you with my bare hands! Do you understand? Do not call here again! You are dead to me!"

After that, my mom did not even wait for my reply. She hung up immediately.

I did not want to bother my family or to hurt anyone. I miss my younger brothers. I was an apostate to them. In their eyes, I am now shameful to them, like a scar on their faces that they wish they could have removed!

I understand that, and I love them. If killing me will lead them to Christ, I am ready! I hope there is a way.

Nancy and I faced difficulties settling into our new country. Everything was so alien to us. As we travelled and visited various churches, many people encouraged me to become a minister or pastor, but I did not feel that was my calling. I was not convinced that God was directing me to be a full-time pastor, at least not yet. I felt somewhat drawn to being a tent-maker pastor.[2] As seemed so often the case, God had other plans for me.

My closest Christian mentor, a pastor I refer to as my spiritual father, told me that if I wanted to serve God, I needed to serve Him alone. I told him I was not ready to do so and that I needed God to call me personally to convince me that I am to be a full-time minister. My spiritual father told me that he was praying and was convinced that one day I would become a full-time minister.

On the night before this talk, I was reading a book which told a unique story. It was about a man who wanted certainty from God about a particular issue. Meanwhile, his friend became convinced that that he knew God's will. However, the man seeking God's will proposed a strange condition for his friend, "If your word is from God, I will consider it a contract. But, I want this contract to be signed by two witnesses."

I did not understand what he meant and did not continue reading that book, but I liked the idea and shared it with my spiritual father, who did not oppose the idea.

The next day, while I was in a shopping mall, a guy whom I had not met before came to me, and asked to pray for me!

I agreed, politely. I wondered whether he was an evangelist who wanted to preach to me. But, he did not preach to me. Rather, he simply prayed that God would call me into full-time ministry!

At this point I began to wonder whether this was the second witness that I had insisted upon earlier to my friend. I was still not sure.

But, after I walked a few hundred feet further in the shopping mall, I encountered another evangelist—who also asked to pray for me! And, I was astounded when he prayed *exactly the same prayer* the first man.

Now, I was sure. I said, "Hallelujah to the Lord. These are the two witnesses. From today, Lord, I am dedicated to working for you."

God is good!

1. I have two brothers. One is 11 years younger than I, and the other 13 years younger.
2. In the early church, some believers conducted their ministry while serving in a secular vocation rather than as professional clergy. Paul himself joined Priscilla and Aquila in doing so for a time, as a tentmaker; a detail reported in Acts 18:3.

10

TOURISTIC BROCHURE

You are of your father the devil, and your will is to do your father's desires...

— JOHN 8:44

Islam in the West is not like Islam in the Middle East. Islam in the West is far more sneaky. When I came from Egypt, I found that they have what basically amounts to a shiny "Touristic Brochure of Islam." This phrase is my own terminology, so far as I know. This brochure is simple; it says that Islam is innocent and one of the most peaceful religions in the world. It gives all the rights to women, animals, and all of creation. Also, it says that whoever tries to criticize Islam is "islamophobic," and discriminates against the Islamic community. And, do you know what? Many people in the West believe them!

In my opinion, the West today is like a man who got a baby anaconda snake and started to feed it, thinking that feeding it would get it to love and respect him. But the problem is that, with this anaconda, you quite literally have a monster in the house. Once it becomes big and strong, the first person it will attack is the person who took care of it and tried to nurture it.

Look at the world today, cities like London in the UK and Malmö in Sweden. Islam invades all these areas under the name of peace and freedom. Actually, today Islam has built parallel societies that have their own Islamic internal police or security, laws, and culture, which is one of the most dangerous things in these countries. In 2017, according to Thornberg from Säpo, which is the national security police, there were around 3,000 violent extremists in Sweden. Some 2,000 of those are believed to have Islamist motives, and the remaining originate from far-right and far-left movements.

A 2010 Säpo report estimated the number of violent Islamist extremists in the country at 200. From 2010 to 2017 they grew from 200 to 2000—a 900% increase over a period of just ten years! This statistic should frighten every Swede, and cause the people of other countries to take warning.

I can easily list more than 120 militant Muslim groups. ISIS[1] is not alone; it is merely one among many.

Here is the trick: Islam has many contradictions that Muslims leverage to their advantage when working to increase the influence and control of Islam in the world. Let's take a subject like freedom in Islam or apostasy as an example. Ask any Imam in any country, especially if you are in a non-Muslim majority country, the following questions and you will receive an emphatic "no" to each one:

- Does Islam deny the freedom of belief?
- Does Islam force people to believe in it?
- Does Islam say that whoever leaves Islam (i.e., becomes apostate) should be killed?
- Does Islam say that anyone should kill any convert?
- Does Islam want to force people's hearts to worship Allah?

But, the questions and their answers are misleading, because the Quran and the Islamic traditions provide a way out of each of these points despite also confirming the opposite. Let us, then, take a closer look. Imagine asking an imam the first one, "Does Islam deny the freedom of belief?"

The Imam will probably say, "No!" and then he may quote the following two verses from the Quran:

There shall be no compulsion in [acceptance of] the religion. The right course has become clear from the wrong. So, whoever disbelieves in Taghut and believes in Allah has grasped the most trustworthy handhold with no break in it. And Allah is Hearing and Knowing."[2]

And say, 'The truth is from your Lord, so whoever wills—let him believe; and whoever wills—let him disbelieve...'[3]

These verses look so open-minded and full of freedom, but they contain a trick. Let's cross-examine the first one:

- Many Islamic scholars agree that this verse refers to the "People of the Book[4] who converted to their religion before its corruption; in which case they pay the *jizya* (tribute)." Other scholars state that the verse was abrogated[5] by the verses of jihad, and that all the people of the world should be called to Islam. If any of them refuse to become Muslims, or refuse to pay the *jizya* (in the case of People of the Book), they should be fought against until they are killed. As Surat at-Tawba (Quran chapter 9), verse 5 states, *"So, when the sacred months are over, slay the idolaters wherever you find them. Take them captive, beseige them, and lie in wait for them in every place of ambush. But if they repent and establish the prayer, and pay the poor-tax, let them go their way."*
- The majority of scholars agree that these verses abrogate each other while some clarified that they do not. The latter group took the opinion that both verses remain in effect but just refer to *distinctions among the Muslim's status and ability*, namely, whether they are able to fight or if they are weak. If they are able to fight, these scholars said, they should fight until they force the enemies into Islam

or into paying the *jizyah*—if they are the People of the
Book. In other words, there is no compulsion in religion
unless the Muslims are in a position to exert compulsion.

- This was the opinion of Ibn Taymiyyah in *Aṣ-Ṣārim al-
  Maslūl ʿalā Shātim ar-Rasūl* (221), Ibn Baz in *Majmū ʾal-
  Fatāwa* (3/ 189-194), and Ibn Kathīr in his Tafsīr.

So, what are the verses of jihad that seem to have abrogated—
that is, canceled—the verse that states there is no compulsion in religion? The main one is Q9:5 that was quoted in italics just above. But
they also include the following,

> O Prophet, fight against the disbelievers and the hypocrites and be
> harsh upon them. And their refuge is Hell, and wretched is that
> destination.[6]

> He says, O you who have believed, fight those adjacent to you of the
> disbelievers and let them find your harshness. And know that Allah
> is with the righteous.[7]

In fact, it is well known among most Islamic scholars that
compulsion really is a key component of Islam's program and right
in the world—no matter what they say to outsiders. The *Ṣaḥīḥ* of al-
Bukhārī is the most respected collection of hadith, perhaps second
in authority only to the Quran itself. It reports on the sometimes
favorable results of compulsion,

> The Prophet said, "Allah wonders at those people who will enter
> Paradise in chains," meaning prisoners brought in chains to the
> Islamic state, then they embrace Islam sincerely and become right-
> eous, and are entered among the people of Paradise."[8]

Not only is compulsion a key element to bring people *into* Islam,
it is also an essential strategy to keep people from *leaving*. Notice the
discussion of Islam's punishments for apostasy, also from *Ṣaḥīḥ al-
Bukhārī*,

Allah's Apostle said, "The blood of a Muslim who confesses that none has the right to be worshipped but Allah and that I am His Apostle cannot be shed except in three cases: In *qisas* [i.e., retaliation] for murder, a married person who commits illegal sexual intercourse, and the one who reverts from Islam [i.e., becomes apostate], and leaves the Muslims."[9]

It is further reported in *Saḥīḥ al-Bukhārī* that,

Ali burnt some people and this news reached Ibn 'Abbās, who said, "Had I been in his place I would not have burnt them, as the Prophet said, 'Don't punish (anybody) with Allah's punishment.' No doubt, I would have killed them, for the Prophet said, 'If somebody (a Muslim) discards his religion, kill him.'"[10]

And again,

A man embraced Islam and then reverted back to Judaism. Mu'adh bin Jabal came and saw the man with Abū Mūsā. Mu'adh asked, "What is wrong with this (man)?" Abū Mūsā replied, "He embraced Islam and reverted back to Judaism." Mu'adh said, "I will not sit down unless you kill him (as it is) the verdict of Allah and His Apostle."[11]

Can you now see? The imam will not tell you all of the important details I've just explained to you. He will just share with you the verse and the cute opinion of the Touristic Islamic Brochure, as I call it, to make you think that Islam respects your freedom to believe as your conscience and rational mind lead you.

Now, let's turn to consider the second verse quoted above, Q18:29. This verse, likewise, seems to respect individual conscience in matters of religious belief. But, the imam will probably not complete the verse when quoting it to you. Why not? See the entire verse quoted here,

And say, "The truth is from your Lord, so whoever wills - let him believe; and whoever wills - let him disbelieve." *Indeed, We have prepared for the wrongdoers a fire whose walls will surround them. And if they call for relief, they will be relieved with water like murky oil, which scalds [their] faces. Wretched is the drink, and evil is the resting place.*[12]

Now, the eternal lake of fire, into which those whose names are not written in the Book of Life (i.e., "the Lamb's book of life, the Lamb who was slain before the foundation of the world," Rev 13:8) is clearly presented in the Bible in Revelation 20:15. However, its mention at that point is stated as a fact in a report of John's vision from Jesus. It is not presented in the form of an obvious threat against unbelievers as is done in the Quran verse above.

To confirm that the Quran's mention of this detail in Q18:29 is intended as a threat, consider the report of Ibn al-Abbās, who is always thought to be one of the most trustworthy and authentic in his reports. He relates, from Muhammad himself,

It is narrated by Ibn al-Abbās his opinion on this verse, where he says: Who God will for him to believe, he believes, and whom God will for him disbelieve, he disbelieves. "And you do not will except that Allah wills—Lord of the worlds." [Surah at-Takwīr (Quran chapter 81), verse 29], and this is not an allowance from God of disbelief for who wills and belief for who wants, but *it is a threat and intimidation.*[13]

So, the context of the first part of the verse, which when presented alone looks very respectful, demonstrates that it is not really about freedom of religion at all, but rather a threat and intimidation against those who do not submit to Islam. Therefore, it would be simply incorrect for anyone to use this verse as proof that Islam respects freedom of choice or conscience in matters of religious belief.

Islam and Politics in the West:

One of the major things that I can observe in the West is how Islam deals with politics and how they are going quickly in the direction of Islamization. Islamization is "A political term denoting the process of increasing the influence of Islam in various spheres of state policy and public life, as well as the process of increasing the number of people professing Islam in a particular region or country."[14]

The standard Muslim position, based upon that of Muhammad himself, is that the whole earth is for the Muslims and should properly be under the control and domination of Muslims. This position is clear in many sources, but to take just one example, as-Sa'di notes in his commentary on Surat an-Nūr 24:55,

> God promised those who came with *imān* (belief) and righteous and correct actions from this *ummah* ("nation") that He would cause them to be successors upon the earth, so that they are the ones in authority and in charge of the affairs. Further that He would establish their religion, that which He was pleased with for them, which is the religion of Islam which gained ascendancy over all of the religions. He was pleased with it for this *ummah*, due to its excellency, nobility and His favors upon it in that He enabled them to establish it and to establish its laws and prescriptions, relating both to manifest and non-manifest matters, upon themselves and others, so that the people of the other religions and the rest of the unbelievers are conquered and humbled.

In order to safeguard against encroaching abuses, I believe that it is important for people in the West to understand Islam's main operating principles when it comes to relationships with non-Muslims and society in general. So, I will conclude this chapter with some key points of summary.

Principle of Governance (*al-hakemiah*)

Muslims believe that Allah is sovereign. The Islamic political system is based on a belief that Allah is the Creator and Lord of the whole universe and everything in it. This would mean that sovereignty over all of humankind rightfully belongs to Allah, and no human or nonhuman power could control or decide any of the human affairs. As the Quran says,

Is it not His to create and to govern?[15]

...Legislation is not but for Allah. He has commanded that you worship no one except Him. That is the correct religion, but most of the people do not know.[16]

We have sent you the Book in Truth that you (O Prophet) might judge between men, as guided by Allah.[17]

If any fail to judge by (the light of) what Allah has revealed, they are (no better than) unbelievers ... they are the wrongdoers ... they are those who rebel.[18]

Do they not see that We are advancing in the land, diminishing it by its borders on all sides? Allah judges, and no one has the power to reverse His judgement. He is swift in reckoning.[19]

Whatever it be wherein ye differ the decision thereof is with Allah: Such is Allah my Lord: in Him I trust and to Him I turn.[20]

O you who believe! Obey Allah and obey the Apostle and those charged with authority among you. If ye differ in anything among yourselves refer it to Allah and His Apostle if ye do believe in Allah and the Last Day: that is best and most suitable for final determination. Hast thou not turned thy vision to those who declare that they believe in the revelations that have come to thee and to those before thee? Their (real) wish is to resort together for judgment (in their disputes) to the Evil One though they were ordered to reject him. But Satan's wish is to lead them astray far away (from the Right).[21]

Then is it the judgement of [the time of] ignorance they desire? But who is better than Allah in judgement for a people who are certain [in faith].[22]

Ibn Kathīr said in his commentary that no one is allowed to follow any other political law or any other judgement except what God said, that whoever does so is *kafir* (i.e., an infidel), and that Muslims' fighting against him becomes an obligation until he goes back to God's governance. What is the political judgment of God? Ibn Kathīr defines it by saying that when any of the other scriptures disagree, the Quran's word must carry the day. His comments refer to Surat al-Māʿida (Quran chapter 5), verse 48, which states that the book [i.e., the Quran] was revealed in truth, confirming whatever Scripture came before, and is *muhaymin* over those previous scriptures. What does *muhaymin* mean? See the commentary of Ibn Kathīr,

> [A]ccording to Sufyan Ath-Thawri who narrated it from Abū Isḥāq from At-Tamimi from Ibn ʿAbbas. ʿAli bin Abi Talhah reported that Ibn ʿAbbas said, "Muhaymin is, 'the Trustworthy.' Allah says that the Qurʾān is trustworthy over every Divine Book that preceded it." This was reported from ʿIkrimah, Saʿid bin Jubayr, Mujahid, Muhammad bin Kaʿb, ʿAtiyyah, Al-Hasan, Qatadah, ʿAta' Al-Khurasani, As-Suddi and Ibn Zayd. Ibn Jarīr said, "The Qurʾān is trustworthy over the Books that preceded it. Therefore, *whatever in these previous Books conforms to the Qurʾān is true, and whatever disagrees with the Qurʾān is false.*" Al-Walibi said that Ibn ʿAbbas said that Muhayminan means, 'Witness.' Mujahid, Qatadah and As-Suddi said the same. Al-ʿAwfi said that Ibn ʿAbbas said that Muhayminan means, 'dominant over the previous Scriptures.' These meanings are similar, as the word Miuhaymin includes them all. Consequently, the Qurʾān is trustworthy, a witness, and dominant over every Scripture that preceded it. The Glorious Book, which Allah revealed as the Last and Final Book, is the most encompassing, glorious and perfect Book of all times. The Qurʾān includes all the good aspects of the previous Scriptures and even

more, which no previous Scripture ever contained. This is why Allah made it trustworthy, a witness and dominant over all Scriptures. Allah promised that He will protect the Qur'ān and swore by His Most Honorable Self.[23]

So, you see, in any disagreement, whether theological or on any legal question, the Quran must prevail. Unless you understand this critical fact about the Islamic worldview, you will not be able to understand the plans that Islam has for your life.

The Islamic State (Caliphate and Consultation)

Khalifa (known in English as caliph) is a man considered by Sunnis to be a successor to the prophet Muhammad and a leader of the entire global Muslim community. The idea of caliph, whose role is as the chief deputy of Allah in the world, exercising his authority through and for the benefit of the faithful Muslims, has its origins in the Quran and in the sunna of Muhammad. For example,

> God has promised those of you who have attained to faith and do righteous deeds that, of a certainty, He will make them Khalifa on earth, even as He caused [some of] those who lived before them to become Khalifa; and that, of a certainty, He will firmly establish for them the religion which He has been pleased to bestow on them; and that, of a certainty, He will cause their erstwhile state of fear to be replaced by a sense of security [seeing that] they worship Me [alone], not ascribing divine powers to aught beside Me. But all who, after [having understood] this, choose to deny the truth – it is they, they who are truly iniquitous![24]

The commentaries clarify the verse's meaning. *Tafsir al-Sa'di*'s explanation of this verse states,

> This is one of his sincere virtues, whose interpretation and revelation have been seen. He promised those who performed faith and good deeds from this nation *to be Khalifa in the land, They are the*

caliphs in it, who rules on it, and that they can have their religion, *which is the religion of Islam,* which *is over top of all religions,* for the virtue, honor and God's grace on this Ummah, *so they will be able to establish it (Islam),* and *to set up its manifest and internal laws, in themselves and others, because people of other religions and other infidels are miserable and humiliated.* [25]

Tafsīr aṭ-Ṭabarī, another major early and widely respected commentary on the Quran, states about this verse,

> *He will make them Khalifa on earth:* Allah will let them (Muslims) the land of Mushrekeen (disbelievers) from Arab and Ajam (Non-Arabic Speakers), so *they become its kings and politicians.* [26]

Continuing on, another commentary called *Tafsīr al-Baghāwī* states,

> Ibn al-Abbās said: The land will be expanded for them until they rule it and their religion (Islam) will be over other religions.

Tafsir Ibn Kathīr further states,

> This is a promise from Allah to His Messenger that *He would cause his Ummah to become successors on earth, i.e., they would become the leaders and rulers of mankind.* [27]

In the *Saḥiḥ* it was recorded that the Messenger of Allah said:

> Allah showed me the earth and I looked at the east and the west. The dominion of my *ummah* will reach everywhere I was shown. [28]

Finally, for now, Ibn Kathīr recorded in *Al-bidāya wa-l-nihāya* that 'Uthmān ibn Affān said, "God can plant with the Sultan 'the Commander of Ummah' greater than what He would plant by the Quran." Taken together, these reports and traditions should help us understand the standard Muslim view of who should be in control of all the people and governments of the world.

Consultation

Deliberations by the caliphates, most notably the Rashidun Caliphate[29] were not democratic in the modern sense. Rather, decision-making power in their time lay with a council of notable and trusted companions of Muhammad and representatives of various tribes (most of them selected or elected within their tribes), and these people—at least according to the later traditions that have reached us—were required to be people who knew the Quran and Sunnah well.

Traditional Sunni Islamic lawyers agree that *Majlis ash-Shūrā* (a council composed of those mentioned above) advised the caliph. The importance of this council is premised by the following verses of the Quran:

...those who answer the call of their Lord and establish the prayer, and *who conduct their affairs by Shūrā.*[30]

...consult them (the people) in their affairs. Then when you have taken a decision (from them), put your trust in Allah.[31]

Al-Bukhārī said in his *Saḥiḥ*, book *al-i'tisām bi-l-kitāb wa-l-sunnah* ("Holding on Quran and Sunna"), in the chapter on "those who conducts their affairs by *shurā*" Surah Shura 42:39:

Imams or *khulafa'* [that is, caliphs] after the prophet used to consult the trustworthy scholars of *ahl al-ḥāl wa-l-'aqad* [i.e., a "consultation board"] in what is allowed as a rule in Islam in order to choose the easiest way, but if the matter is clarified in the Quran and Sunnah, they never cross the limits but rather just adapt to what the Prophet taught."

Sharia (i.e., Islamic Law)

The word *shari'a* is often translated as "Islamic law," but the word more literally means simply "the pathway," or "path to the watering hole," and is understood by Muslims to the pathway laid out by Allah that must be followed. Verses and Islamic traditions that reference or allude to the *shari'a* include,

> And We have sent down to you *the Book as clarification for all things and as guidance* and mercy and good tidings for the Muslims.[32]

> Never was the Quran a narration invented, but a confirmation of what was before it and *a detailed explanation of all things* and guidance and mercy for a people who believe...[33]

> So *govern between the people by that which God has revealed [i.e., Islam]* and follow not their vain desires, beware of them in case they seduce you from just some part of that which God has revealed to you.[34]

> *O you who believe! Obey God, and obey the messenger and then those among you who are in authority; and if you have a dispute concerning any matter, refer it to God and the Messenger's rulings,* if you are (in truth) believers in God and the Last Day. That is better and more seemly in the end.[35]

> Muhammad said, "I have left behind two things, you will never go astray as long as you hold fast onto them; the Quran and Sunnah."[36]

When considering *shari'a*, it is important to remember that, in the Muslim worldview, everyone in the world must live and abide by the *shari'a*; it is not just something meant to govern Muslims. Rather, Muslims are to be the adminstrators, the arbiters, and the rulers.

Jihad

According to Ibn al-Qayyim in *Zād al-Miad* and Ibn Hajar in *Fatḥ al-Bārī*, the classifications of jihad are as follows:

Jihad an-Nafs (fought against the self; an internal struggle)

- Learning your religion and how to apply it in your life, then teaching it, and having the patience and persistence to do so.

Jihad ash-Shaytan (fought against Devil)

- Fighting against all false desires and slanderous doubts in faith that he throws towards the servant

Jihad al-Fasiqūn (fought gainst the hypocrites, i.e., professed believers who are not true)

- Fighting against hypocrites with one's self, one's wealth, one's tongue, and one's heart

Jihad Al Kuffār (fought against infidels, i.e., non-Muslims)

- Fighting against infidels with one's self, one's wealth, one's tongue, and one's heart
- The Messenger of Allah (i.e., Muhammad) said, "Whoever amongst you sees an evil, he must change it with *his hand*; if he is unable to do so, then with *his tongue*; and if he is unable to do so, then with *his heart*; and that is *the weakest form of Faith*."[37]
- This category of jihad includes all manner of actions and attitudes employed to give Islam the upper hand in every part of life and society. One example of the intentional systematic diminishing of non-Muslims can be seen in the following strong hadith: "Do not greet the Jews and the Christians before they greet you and when you meet any one of them on the roads force him to go to the narrowest part of it."[38] In fact, in *Saḥīḥ Muslim*, there is an entire chapter called "the book of greeting" (*salam*), dedicated only to the topic of how to greet different

people. In addition to forbidding Muslims from starting a greeting of a Jew or a Christian, it also instructs Muslims how to answer their greeting.[39]

These points are only a high-level summary of the concept of jihad. Muslims, when presenting their shiny "Touristic Brochure" version of Islam to people in the West, will often emphasize the first type of jihad, the one which is focused upon an internal struggle to live a good and moral life. But, this aspect of jihad only came into strong emphasis in more modern times. And, in truth, the more aggressive external forms such as fighing against non-Muslims really remains the core and primary meaning of jihad as understood by Muslim scholars and many everyday devout Muslims outside of their promotional "Touristic Brochure" even to this day.[40]

New Methods of Islamic Groups

Today, Islam is not strong as it once was, so Muslims cannot apply the Law of Allah as Islam requires. Therefore Muslims feel a need to become strong again, and to do this, they employ various methods, including

1. Focusing on establishing the correct understanding of Islam, that is, one that aligns with the understanding of Muhammad's companions
2. Controlling mosques as much as they can, so they can spread and lead Muslims—especially Salafism
3. Creating a parallel society in foreign countries
4. Having more children, as is generally recommended in Islam and is needed to have a bigger population
5. More involvement and spreading out through political groups to gain authority in parliament or even a municipality board. (Like the Muslim Brotherhood-and Salafism recently)
6. Being more involved in social activities to win people's love.

7. Focusing more on da'wa to the West and Africa. (the Salafi approach)

8. Focusing on specific areas in the Muslim countries and outside it and sometimes having control over these areas.

9. Trying to capture any opportunity to prove their existence and to apply any of the Shari'a laws or even impose a Islam culturally.

10. Use democracy as a path to apply Shari'a Law and Islam in business, and through local authorities and political channels.

How to deal with "Islamophobia"

A phobia is an extreme or irrational fear of or aversion to something. I regard *islamophobia* as a reprehensible word, because phobia is a technical medical/psychological term and now it is used whenever we have ideological/identity conflict. Whenever *islamophobia* is said, I doubt the intention of the one who uses it, because it has manipulation built into its structure. In the United States, the law already protects the rights of Muslims and everyone else to speak and exercise their religion freely, and to be free from violence by others. If the law already protects your rights, then why do you add extra law to protect yourself?

---

1. The Islamic State In Syria, also known as *Daesh*, which is an acronym for its name in Arabic.
2. Surat al-Baqarah (Quran chapter 2) verse 256
3. Surat al-Kahf (Quran chapter 18), verse 29
4. People of the Book (Arabic *ahl al-kitāb*) is a Quranic category of people that includes Christians, Jews, and Zoroastrians. Under Islamic conquest, People of the Book are treated differently than ordinary pagans or atheists. Unlike the latter category, who must choose either to become Muslim or to be killed, People of the Book are permitted a third choice, namely, to live in subjugation to the Muslims and in submission to Islamic law, including annual payment of the *jizya*.
5. Abrogation (Arabic: *naskh*), the idea that some Quran verses supersede and cancel out others, is a very important principle in Islamic jurisprudence. When two verses disagree with each other, Islamic scholars look for information on

which one was revealed to Muhammad later. Then, the later verse is understood
to have abrogated the earlier one.

6. Surat at-Tawba (Quran chapter 9), verse 73
7. Surat at-Tawba (Quran chapter 9), verse 123
8. *Saḥiḥ al-Bukhārī*, Vol. 4, Book 52, number 254. M. Muḥsin Khan (tr.)
9. Ibid., 9:83:17; see also *Saḥiḥ Muslim* 16:4152 and 16:4154
10. Ibid., 4:52:260
11. Ibid., 9:89:271
12. Emphasis added
13. *Tafsir aṭ-Ṭabarī*, commentary on Q18:29; emphasis added
14. Emilia Alaverdov and Aytekin Demircioğlu. *Handbook of Research on Ethnic, Racial, and Religious Conflicts and Their Impact on State and Social Security.* 2021. Chapter 1.
15. Surat al-Araf (Quran chapter 7) verse 54
16. Surat Yusuf (Quran chapter 12), verse 40
17. Surat An-Nisā' (Quran chapter 4), verse 105
18. Surat al-Mā'ida (Quran chapter 5), verses 44-47
19. Surat Ar-Ra'd (Quran chapter 13), verse 41
20. Surat Ash-Shūrā (Quran chapter 42), verse 10
21. Surat An-Nisā' (Quran chapter 4), verses 59-60
22. Surat al-Mā'ida (Quran chapter 5), verse 50
23. Ibn Kathīr, *Tafsir*, (on Mā'ida:48). Referenced at Quran.com.
24. Surat An-Nūr (Quran chapter 24), verse 55
25. Emphasis added
26. Emphasis added
27. Emphasis added
28. Ibn Kathīr, *Tafsīr*; this tradition is also reported in *Saḥiḥ Muslim*
29. The *Rashidūn* were the four caliphs immediately following Muhammad. They are titled *rashidūn*, which means "rightly-guided," because it is believed that their governance was protected from error by Allah in a special way.
30. Surat Ash-Shūrā (Quran chapter 42), verse 38; emphasis added
31. Surat Ali 'Imrān (Quran chapter 3), verse 159
32. Surat an-Nahl (Quran chapter 16), verse 89; emphasis added
33. Surat Yūsuf (Quran chapter 12), verse 111; emphasis added
34. Surat al-Mā'ida (Quran chapter 5), verse 49; emphasis added
35. Surat an-Nisā' (Quran chapter 4), verse 59; emphasis added
36. *Saḥiḥ Muslim* 2408
37. *Sunan an-Nasa'ī* 5008
38. *Saḥiḥ Muslim* 2167a
39. *Saḥiḥ Muslim* 4030
40. For an excellent historical and scholarly presentation of the topic of jihad, I recommend David Cook's now-standard work, *Understanding Jihad* (University of California Press, 2005).

11

IN SERVICE OF THE TRUE KING

...and what you have heard from me in the presence of many witnesses entrust to faithful men, who will be able to teach others also

— 2 TIMOTHY 2:2

A new season in my life started the moment the second man prayed for me in the shopping mall, answering my request to God for confirmation by two witnesses. Instantly, I thought I would be able to preach and teach everywhere since I had become dedicated to the Lord. I expected that many people would ask me to serve, and that I was going to be of immediate and dramatic use to the kingdom of God!

However, it quickly became evident that nobody was welcoming me to preach or teach. Even my spiritual father started to feel anxious, and he was trying to encourage me, but still, there was no hope.

At that time, Nancy and I had no place to live except a storage room in a summer house in a forest that is remote—around 40 minutes from the closest train station. This was really hard! It was terrifying to go home late for any reason because this meant that I had to walk in the light of the moon as there was no other light, as it was a forest. Our only way not to feel afraid was to praise and sing to God all the way back home.

I still remember one day when we had to go home late, and it was winter, the temperature was -12 °F, and Nancy and I were very tired. Nancy, being scared of the snakes and wild boars that roamed that forest, was trying to walk close beside me. Then, I heard the sound of Nancy crying in the darkness.

"Why are you crying? What's up?" I asked.

"Nothing," she answered.

I persisted, "Nancy, I hear that you are crying, tell me what happened?"

She said, "Nothing, I am just cold." She was crying because her gloves were not sufficient for such a low temperature.

So, I took off my gloves and put them on her hand over her own gloves.

"But what about you?" she asked.

I said, "I feel warm. It's not that cold!" It was not true except in an extremely relative sense (I probably felt warmer than I would if it had been minus 50!), but I needed her not to feel guilty that I took off my gloves for her.

We were almost isolated in this house from everything around us. Then, when I prayed a lot about why God was not using us as I had been hoping and expecting, I sensed the answer. Simply, I was not ready. Really, that was one of the great benefits that God used this place where we lived to be our training camp. We were there, and I had nothing to do but read my Bible, pray, and read different books, and I think that this is precisely what God wanted. We stayed in this training camp for a whole year.

But at the end of this year, God opened the door, and suddenly, many people started to invite me to teach and share my experience.

Around that time, I decided that I needed to study more, as I do not accept speaking without knowledge or just because I read a lot. I learned, even in Salafism, that "whoever has his book as his teacher will do mistakes more than corrections:", But it was not easy to find the right place and the right education for me. I was guided by my mentor in Egypt to an apologetics academy where I studied for a whole year. But this was not enough, and I wanted to be specialized in what I love, which is Christian Islamic Studies. I do not deny that there are many programs, but unfortunately, most of these programs are not strong enough.

One day, a friend of mine called me and asked, "Have you heard of i2 Ministries?"

I said, "No!"

He said, "You want to study and you would love to do that in Christian Islamic Studies, and i2 Ministries has one of the best online universities in the world in this field called MMWU—'Mission Muslim World University.'"

I said, "Wow! Can you give me the link? Can you help me to join? Would they accept me? Are they strong enough?"

He said, "I will connect you to the head of operations."

Well, it happened and I joined; it was an amazing study! I discovered that MMWU indeed has a master's program in ministry with an Islamic Studies concentration with the best teachers in the profession teaching across the different courses. I started in the program, and I was so enthusiastic!

While studying at MMWU, I was amazed to meet hundreds of Christian leaders from all over the world who shared my passion for reaching the Muslim world. In many ways, this became a new family for me. I finally found a place that felt like home with many others with whom I could pray and collaborate with in ministry.

Two years later, I finished my studies, and I am honored now to have become the head of the Arabic language division of MMWU, where I also teach in the English program under my amazing brother and friend, Dr. Joshua Lingel. Through MMWU, I got to know a lot of people: teachers, missionaries, and pastors around the world. It is a blessing to be part of this amazing work they do. After completing my academic work at MMWU, I moved onward to God's Bible School and College (GBSC)—a small school with an amazing heritage (Oswald Chambers, author of the popular devotional *My Utmost For His Highest*, was a teacher there near the time of its founding, and remained a lifelong friend)—to finish the rest of the subjects in my master's program.

Today I am preparing to enter a Ph.D. program while also teaching in different churches and organizations. I also serve as a chaplain in one of the churches. As mentioned already, my master's work focused on the Trinity, and the book I read of Rahmatullah at the beginning of my life is the book that I refuted in my thesis. How amazing is the Lord and his timing?

There are many details that I was not able to write in this book, but maybe one day I will be able to do so. Today I am proud to be called a Christian. Christ is worthy to be followed and to be worshiped.

Having read earlier my reasons to reject the other religions I have followed and tested, I want to present the reader with a similar list showing at least some of the ways in which my questions have been answered and my soul has found peace.

12

A SHORT SUMMARY

Having read earlier my reasons to reject the other religions I have followed and tested, I want to present the reader with a similar list showing at least some of the ways in which my questions have been answered and my soul has found peace.

I do believe in Christianity because (I have endless reasons, but I will try to be brief and precise)

First, I believe that God exists and He is good, holy, and wise infinitely, based upon

- The *cosmological argument.* "In the beginning:" God is immaterial, unlimited in space-time, omnipotent (created from nothing), and He is a person.
- The *teleological argument.* "The Intelligent Designer:" God is omniscient, all-wise, and all-caring
- The *moral argument* says that God is holy, and that He is a person.

Second, I believe in Christianity because I believe that it answers my existential questions (e.g., where, why, and how I should live, and where I will go after die) in a genuine, coherent and applicable way.

Third, I believe that God should be a Tri-unity so that He could be all-loving even before anything was created.

Fourth, I believe the Bible is reliable. In terms of manuscripts, we have 5589 New Testament in Greek, 10,000 in Latin, and 10,000 in an old language (such as Assyrian, Coptic. etc.) with a total of around 25,000 manuscripts.

Fifth, I believe that Christianity is historically reliable and that, historically, Jesus was resurrected—which alone is sufficient to prove that Christianity is true and that there is an afterlife.

Sixth, I believe that the Jesus of the First century, as described in the New and Old Testaments, is reliable and historically proven through eyewitnesses. As such, he is completely above any other Jesus (such as the Jesus of the Jews, the Muslims, the Jehovah's Witnesses, or the Mormons)

Seventh, I believe that Jesus's disciples were strict Jewish monotheists who—*because of his clear teaching about himself,* supported by miracles—included Jesus within the identity of YHWH, Israel's God, over against all others, and had been revealed in 580 scripture references in the 27 books of the New Testament.

Eighth, I believe (as the Bible states) that no person can be saved through his or her deeds, but only through grace, which is God's power to accomplish what we cannot do for ourselves, and the highest manifestation of grace is what Jesus did on the Cross.

Ninth, I believe that the single timeline across the Bible from Genesis to Revelation is so solid and transparent that it could never have happened by chance or without the person of God, who is sovereign, omniscient, and omnipotent.

Tenth, I do not believe that Jesus' disciples would have accepted being killed or jailed for something they had made up or for a myth or had not witnessed for themselves.

Eleventh, I believe that there is an incredible level of coherence to the Bible and all its accounts, with the highest amount of accuracy of a written book—despite the fact that it was written by forty-four different writers in different geographical locations, in different time periods, and from a variety of backgrounds.

Twelfth, if the chance for seven prophecies to be fulfilled in one person is $1/10^{12}$, this would mean that if the whole surface of the earth were covered with coins showing one side, with only a single one turned to the other, my chance to find this one is $1/10^{12}$. That being the case, what can we make of the 333 prophecies happening about one person? How can he not be Jesus Christ, as he claimed?

My message to others after this long journey is that Satan has many faces. These faces could include Islam, Atheism, Agnosticism, Deism, Hinduism, Buddhism, or New Age, but at the end, they are just different ways for Satan to distract you away from the Lord Jesus Christ. As the Bible says: "...He was a murderer from the beginning and did not stand in the truth, because there is no truth in him."[1] Truth vs. Lie, Light vs. Darkness, and Life vs. Death. You and you alone can choose what you want and what you need. It would be intelligent for you not to repeat my mistakes; I wrote a summary after each worldview for you to study and dig deep into. If you found it right, do not waste your time away from Christ because our time with Christ is the only time that counts.

If you find yourself face-to-face with a radical Salafi Muslim, I would like to remind you of three things:

1. This person is made in the image of God.
2. Jesus died for everyone—even this man or woman.
3. And, there is also hope for you to be saved!

Jesus says, "Behold, I stand at the door and knock. If anyone hears my voice and opens the door, I will come in to him" (Revelation 3:20).

---

1. John 8:44

13

THE GREAT COMMISSION

Go therefore and make disciples of all nations, baptizing them in
the name of the Father and of the Son and of the Holy Spirit,
teaching them to observe all that I have commanded you.

— MATTHEW 28:19-20A

P lease take an extended moment to consider the words of
Jesus shown above, commonly called the Great Commission. Notice that Jesus told *every* Christian to help in
completing His work. If you are a Christian, that includes you!

Jesus gave each of us a command to do our part to make sure all
people everywhere have a chance to become His followers. Today,
looking around the world, we see 2 billion Muslims living in every
country of the world. These lost souls encompass nearly 40% of all
non-Christian individuals globally. Reaching the Muslim world with
the Gospel is the final and greatest missions frontier and must be
prioritized as such in every church.

The strange thing is that most Christians do not even seem to
think that we need to take the Gospel to Muslims! When I reflect on
this fact, it makes me weep. I was lost, destined to die in my sins and
spend eternity in Hell! What would have happened to me if no

Christian had ever given me the time of day or made the effort to tell me about Jesus—not the cartoon Jesus of the Quran but the real Jesus of history who loved me, died for my sins, and rose again? A watching world can read between the lines. As one non-Christian said, "If you believe Christianity is true and you are convinced I am on my way to Hell, is it not a great act of hatred for you to ignore sharing with me how to be saved?"

The reality is that 38,000 Muslims die every single day—and 86% of them never get a chance to hear the Gospel. This situation must change!

As a former Salafi Muslim, I grew up knowing that Islam had a practical strategy to take over the world. I participated in this strategy and I saw how it worked. When I became a Christian, I was shocked that the global church did not also have a well-developed and focused strategy to fulfill the Great Commission, especially among Muslims who represent the largest single religion, in terms of number of adherents, after the Christian faith.

From what I have witnessed, it seems that most Christians are afraid or feel ill-equipped to talk to Muslims about Jesus, and that such fear leads them to intentionally skip opportunities to do so, concluding they are too difficult to reach! How, then, is the Great Commission going to be accomplished?

Did Jesus not promise that in these last days, there would be a vast multitude from every tribe, tongue, people, and nation who would turn to Him and be saved (Joel 2:28-32; Revelation 5:9-10, 7:9-17)?

Speaking from my own conversion experience and from what the scriptures tell us, that end-time harvest will **not** happen without mature Christians sharing the Gospel and intentionally discipling new believers (Matthew 24:14; Romans 10:13-14). In other words, it takes a real disciple to make another real disciple.

But the good news is that if all 900 million born-again Christians were to make just one disciple per year, and all those disciples also made one disciple per year, and the trend continued, the *entire world* of 8 billion people could be reached *in just 3 years.*

Reading this book has given you some tools to help you reach

Muslims, but reading is not enough. Yes, other Muslims who are asking the same questions may be moved by my testimony (I certainly hope so!), but that's not enough. Yes, there are probably millions of other Muslims who have come to Christ, but it's not enough. Think of every single lost person out there in the world as if he or she was you, wandering in the darkness. Doesn't that person urgently need to hear some very good news from someone like you?

God tells you and every Christian church to take ownership of their important part in the global initiative to share the Gospel with *every* Muslim (Mark 16:15)!

I have often found it to be the case that, when Christians hear me talking about reaching Muslims, they start thinking about doing so in some far-away place where Muslims live.

However, only 15% of Muslims live in the Middle East, while over a billion Muslims live in Asia, 500 million are in Africa, and 50 million live in Europe. And many people are surprised to learn that only 15% of all the Muslims in the world even speak Arabic!

In fact, it is estimated that today the majority of the global Muslim population actually lives within the immediate vicinity of one of the 5.5 million local churches around the world.[1] This fact means that if every church takes responsibility for reaching all the Muslims local to where they are, then we would have a practical strategy to help finish the Great Commission. I am laboring with a group of faithful men to see these Every Muslim for Christ Initiatives get launched all around the world, and you can also get involved! Here is how:

1. Pray
2. Get trained
3. Train others
4. Share the Gospel

Pray

Commit to Pray Matthew 9:37-38 every day at 9:37.

> Then he (Jesus) said to his disciples, "The harvest is plentiful, but the laborers are few; therefore pray earnestly to the Lord of the harvest to send out laborers into his harvest."

Jesus did NOT say the harvest was not ripe. Actually, He said the opposite. He is telling us that the harvest IS ripe, but the problem is that there are not enough laborers to bring in the harvest. Typically, to work a bigger field, you would need to train and pay more workers. However, Jesus implies that the problem with the lack of workers is primarily a spiritual one, and the main solution is **prayer.** Jesus' strong focus on prayer in this matter shows us that God has chosen to intricately tie the establishment of new workers to the faith-filled cries of His people.

A Matthew 9:37-38 prayer culture must be established in every church and in the heart of every single believer. We need a global unified cry to ascend before the Throne, beckoning God to raise up a multitude of new workers to be thrust into the ripe Muslim fields.

Get Trained

Five verses after Jesus gave this command for the disciples to pray; He commissions them to **go** (Matthew 10:5). Many missiologists describe this sending in Matthew 10 as a missions training exercise to get the disciples ready for their post-Pentecost ministry. This shows us that Jesus desires you to labor in prayer, and the way he will answer your prayer is by getting you ready to be an effective laborer!

I want invite you to join our online school, Mission Muslim World University (MMWU). I personally loved going through this program, and I think you will too! MMWU is designed to raise up a generation of laborers who can lead the charge in finishing the Great Commission among Muslims. Over forty professors have contributed to the program. It is considered by many the most comprehensive curriculum anywhere in the world for equipping Christians to reach Muslims with the Gospel. While solidly academic, that is not all there is to MMWU. Just like Jesus' training in

Matthew 10, the university also emphasizes sharing the Gospel as the true heart of the matter. MMWU also offers a pathway to a master's degree in Christian Ministry with an Islamic Studies concentration that can be completed 100% online. The courses are self-paced, and you can start whenever you want. You can do a single course or the full program. On the next page, I'll help you enroll with a significantly discounted rate.

Train Others

Developing leaders in every country is the keystone of every successful global strategy. So, if we are going to finish the Great Commission, we need the proper leadership in every country. To state it a bit differently, to be a disciple maker, one must learn to be a leader, as discipling implies training others to train others. No matter if you are a student, work in the marketplace, or are in full-time ministry, MMWU will equip you as a leader to train and mobilize others to reach Muslims with the Gospel.

I am extremely proud to be on the leadership team of MMWU, and I am so grateful that you have taken the time to read my book so I want to give you something in return. If you scan the QR code below, you'll find a link to enroll in the *Islam's Issues, Agendas, and the Great Commission* master's course at a 67% discount. I am one of the teachers in the first course, and it would be my great honor to train you in a more comprehensive way!

bit.ly/MMWU_Book_Offer

Share the Gospel

Most importantly, you need to share the Gospel with Muslims. Did you know that talking about Jesus with Muslims is much easier than with atheists or agnostics? Many times, Muslims are waiting to have spiritual conversations just like we are. It is quite normal for people from the Eastern world to have passionate conversations about all subjects in life. Whether friends are trying to pick a restaurant, people are discussing their favorite football teams, or when strangers are discussing religion, Muslims love to engage in a lively discussion. The most important thing is that you steer the first conversation into a spiritual conversation so that you can build your future relationship around "God conversations." Be extremely relational, and extremely intentional. In the book of Acts, Paul never waited for a second conversation before sharing about Jesus, and neither should you. (In the first MMWU course, you will learn some very practical ways to guide conversations with Muslims, and you will gain tools beyond what's in this book that will help you answer questions that may be posed to you.)

Remember: If you have trusted Jesus for the forgiveness of your sins, then you are an anointed ambassador of His with the Spirit of God dwelling inside you. And along with that, Jesus expressly promised that He would always be with you while you labor to complete the Great Commission as He instructed (Matt. 28:20).

Demonstrate to every Muslim the **love** of God, the **power** of God (through prayer), and help them understand the **truth** of the glorious Gospel that is the power of God for the salvation of everyone who believes (Romans 1:16).

Thanks for reading!

Yours In Christ,
Thomas Samuel

---

1. Personal communication with Dr. Joshua Lingel based on information from Todd Johnson, co-director of Gordon-Conwell Theological Seminary's Center for the Study of Global Christianity.

GLOSSARY

Arabic words that may be unfamiliar to some readers are used in this book. Many of the terms below are defined where they first appear in this book, but also here for easy reference.[1]

abrogation (Arabic: *naskh*): Abrogation, the idea that some Quran verses supersede and cancel out others, is a very important principle in Islamic jurisprudence. When two verses disagree with each other, Islamic scholars look for information on which one was revealed to Muhammad later. Then, the later verse is understood to have abrogated the earlier one.

Allah: The Islamic word for God. It is a cognate of the Hebrew word *Elohim*, one of the three words for God that appears in the Bible, but not his personal name. However, for Muslims God's personal name as revealed to Moses (יהוה - YHWH) is unknown. Accordingly, many Muslims consider Allah to be God's name.

da'wa: Literally "invitation," it is the Islamic practice of proselytizing non-Muslims. Da'wa takes many forms, from literature distribution, to dialogues and debates, to street preaching and personal persuasion.

dhimma (pronounced "*thimma*"): An agreement that gives Christians, Jews, and Zoroastrians immunity from being killed by Muslims for the crime of existing, so long as they agree to live with abridged rights as tributaries (paying the *jizya* annually), and to abide by the constricting demands that the Muslims place upon them. The *dhimma* is sometimes called a "pact of protection," because it protects the subjected *dhimmis* from outside threats as well as from Muslims.

dhimmi (pronounced "*thimee*"): A Christian, a Jew, or a Zoroastrian under Islamic rule.

Gospel: The word means, literally, "good news." As used in the New Testament, it refers to the good news that is the Bible's central message, namely, that the penalty for your sins was completely paid by the atoning sacrifice on the Cross of the spotless Passover Lamb, Jesus Christ, and that you can therefore be saved apart from works, by grace, through faith in Him. When capitalized without further reference (i.e., "the Gospel"), this particular good news is signified.

Hadith: Literally "event," a hadith in Islam is a report, typically of something that Muhammad or one of his companions said, or did, or approved, or disapproved. Hadith were gathered in the centuries after Muhammad's death, written down, sorted by topic, and then eventually rated in terms of authenticity. There are six main collections of hadith that are authoritative in Sunnī Islam. When the word is not capitalized (i.e., "hadith"), it typically refers to a single hadith. When capitalized (i.e., "Hadith" or "the Hadith"), the entire body of these reports is usually being referenced.

Hijra: The famous migration, from Mecca to Medina, of the early community of believers in Muhammad's message that, according to Islamic tradition, occurred in 622 AD. The Hijra came to mark the beginning of the Islamic calendar, which is designated by the abbreviation A.H. Thus, the year 622 AD became for the early community the year 1 AH.

ibn: Arabic word for "[the] son of." For example, "John ibn Joe" would mean "John, the son of Joe." Sometimes, *ibn* is abbreviated *b.*, as in *John b. Joe*. It means the same thing.

jihad: Fighting or struggling in the way of Allah. The primary meaning of jihad has always been military conquest, but it also includes other initiatives to establish Islam's political and spiritual dominance over territory and people. Thus, jihad can include *da'wa*, or it can include efforts to get a position of influence in a secular government or organization, or efforts to establish Islamic law by getting non-Muslims to abide by it (for example, by requiring others to act in compliance with, or deference to, Islam's speech, morality, or dietary codes).

jizya: A tax that is required to be paid by all dhimmis to the Muslim authorities every year under Islamic law.

khalifa (Arabic: خليفة): The Arabic word for caliph. It is a title which means "successor," "ruler," or "leader." Khalifa most commonly refers to the leader of a caliphate but is also used as a title among various Islamic religious groups and others. Khalifa is sometimes also pronounced "kalifa." There were four khalifas after Muhammad died, beginning with Abū Bakr, then 'Umar, then 'Uthmān, then 'Alī ibn Abī Tālib.

muṣhaf (pronounced *"moose-hoff"*): A bound book, with pages

People of the Book (Arabic *ahl al-kitāb*): A Quranic category of people that includes Christians, Jews, and Zoroastrians. Under Islamic conquest, People of the Book are treated differently than pagans or atheists. Unlike the latter category of people, who must choose either to become Muslim or to be killed, People of the Book are permitted a third choice, namely, to live in subjugation to the Muslims and submission to Islamic law, including (among many other restrictions) annual payment of the *jizya*.

Salafi: A member of, or adherent to, Salafism—a movement of Muslims seeking to conform to the practices of the *salaf aṣ-ṣāliḥ*, the pious predecessors or members of the first three generations of pious believers during and after Muhammad's lifetime. The most radical Muslims are Salafis.

Shia: The second largest group of Muslims, Shia Islam predominates in Iran, Yemen, Bahrain, and several other countries. The Sunni-Shia divide developed gradually in the earliest centuries of Islam. Shia Muslims understand the succession of authority after Muhammad to have continued through his family. Shia make up about 15% of Muslims in the world today.

sunna: the example of Muhammad and, to a certain extent, the pious believers from his generation and the two following generations.

Sunni: The largest portion of Muslims today. Sunni Muslims model their life and practice after the *sunna* of Muhammad and his companions, as understood from the Hadith and other sources from the early centuries. Sunnis make up about 85% of Muslims in the world today.

surah (or **surat**): A chapter of the Quran

tafsir: A commentary explaining the meaning of the Quran

ummah: Literally "people" or "community," it is the global body of Muslims, collectively

---

1. Glossary © 2024 D. Brubaker

Join the global community

MISSION MUSLIM WORLD UNIVERSITY

Mission Muslim World University is the most comprehensive online school available in Christian missions to Muslims and Islamic studies, offering a pathway to a fully online, fully accredited MA degree in ministry with an Islamic studies concentration. Over 40 world-class professors have contributed to this robust nine-course curriculum.

As a "thank you" for reading this book, we are offering you admission into the first course, *Islam's Issues, Agendas, and the Great Commission,* for just $290. Tuition for this Master's level course is normally $880. Follow this link/QR code to enroll today!

bit.ly/MMWU_Book_Offer

MMWU PROFESSORS

Joshua Lingel	Georges Houssney
Jay Smith	Al-Fadi
Josh McDowell	Nabeel Qureshi
Sasan Tavassoli	Darrell Bock
Carl Ellis	Daniel Wallace
Roland Muller	Tom Doyle
Robert Coleman	Michael Bird
Mark Durie	Michael Brown
J.P. Moreland	Robert Bowman
Mike Shipman	Jesse Digges
Daniel Brubaker	Gary Habermas
Beth Grove	Sudhakar Mondithoka
Tony Weedor	David Talley
David Cook	Joel Richardson
Elsie Maxwell	Mike Licona
Sean McDowell	Stephen Venable
William Wagner	Bill Nikides
James White	Adam Simnowitz
David Wood	Tomas Samuel
Richard Bauckham	Mike Tisdell

For more information about MMWU, visit mmwu.org | i2ministries.org

About the Author

Fernando Sáez is currently Director of the Pablo Neruda Foundation in Santiago, Chile. As a biographer, he has published *La Hormiga: Biografía de Delia del Carril* [The Ant: A Biography of Delia del Carril] and *La vida intranquila: Biografía de Violeta Parra* [The Restless Life: A Biography of Violeta Parra]. He has also published the novels *Atentado final* [Final Attempt], *Aire visible* [Visible Air], and *La novela de Amanda Romo* [The Novel of Amanda Romo], as well as the play *Abandonada* [Abandoned] and the short story collection *Guantes amarillos* [Yellow Gloves].

About the Translator

Jessica Sequeira has published the novel *A Furious Oyster*, the story collection *Rhombus and Oval*, the essay collection *Other Paradises: Poetic Approaches to Thinking in a Technological Age* and the hybrid work *A Luminous History of the Palm*. She has translated more than twenty books of poetry and prose by Latin American authors, and in 2019 was awarded the Premio Valle-Inclán for her translation of Sara Gallardo's *Land of Smoke*. Currently she lives between Chile and the UK, where she is based at the Centre of Latin American Studies at the University of Cambridge.